Think and Grow Rich for Inventors

John Rizvi, Esq.

Registered Patent Attorney

Copyright © 2017 John Rizvi, Esq.

All rights reserved. This book or any portion thereof may not be reproduced or used in any manner whatsoever without the express written permission of the publisher except for the use of brief quotations in a book review.

First Printing, 2017

ISBN: 978-1-63443-736-3

Most names have been changed to maintain privacy of the individuals referenced within these pages.

Praise

Kevin Harrington
— Original "shark" on the hit
TV Series _Shark Tank®_, and
the inventor of the infomercial
and _As Seen on TV_. Kevin has
successfully launched over 500
products resulting in more than
$5 billion in sales worldwide.

 I know a thing or two about successfully launching new products.

And over the years, I've worked with a lot of patent attorneys. Most of them speak in legalese and, quite frankly, are hard to understand and have no practical sense for business.

John Rizvi is different. He is plain spoken and down to earth. Not only does he know patent law, but as an Adjunct Professor he has perfected the art of teaching it to law students and other attorneys for almost 20 years.

He has a knack for explaining difficult legal concepts in plain English.

In fact, that is why I asked John to write the chapter on patents in my new book. John is the real deal.

In his book, *Think and Grow Rich for Inventors*, John tells the inspiring story of a client of his that dropped out of medical school and launched a new surgical tool, selling his patent for a $100 million dollars.

Think and Grow Rich is the single best-selling self-help book of all time. And John takes the teachings of this classic by Napoleon Hill and demystifies the principles of success for the inventor.

If you have an idea and the drive to develop that idea to its limits, you can't go wrong by getting *Think and Grow Rich for Inventors*. **""**

Table of Contents

Dedication & Acknowledgments

This book is dedicated to my father, a remarkable engineer that infused in me a lifelong passion for science and technology and an appreciation for those brave individuals that dare to create something new from nothing;

To my mother, for never allowing me to feel that there was anything that I could not do;

To my wife, Saba, for her love, support and unwavering belief in my success particularly in those times when I could scarcely muster the courage to believe in myself.

To my family, friends, peers and mentors, who stood behind me on this journey and support me still to this day;

And finally, to all of those inventors, entrepreneur, and creative geniuses that have inspired and paved the way for others with their pioneering spirit to continue to change and shape the world we live in, and especially those who chose me to help them for a time on their individual journeys.

Foreword

Think and Grow Rich, by Napoleon Hill, became the single best-selling self-help book in history. Debuting in 1937, Hill revealed the commonalities among over 500 of the greatest minds in modern business and innovation, distilling these singular characteristics into 13 essential steps to achieving success and financial freedom. Since *Think and Grow Rich* moved into the public domain, a number of spin-off titles have been produced, targeting different segments of the population.

I came to know Napoleon Hill's landmark work while I was in law school, studying it relentlessly between general law and my intended specialization of patent law. What attracted me to *Think and Grow Rich* was the powerful glimpse he offered into the mind of innovators. Part of the attraction stemmed from the idea that these concepts are replicable and available to anyone with the strength of will to put them into practice. The book became my personal Bible, one which I checked out from the library so often and lingered so long over that I amassed some substantial library fines.

As I look back over my career and my rise to operating my own private patent law firm, I see clearly how Hill's seminal work influenced and shaped my movements at every turn. It has always been my dream to work with innovators and inventors, to act as the "spiritual midwife" of their ideas and help them secure and maintain the rights to the results of their labor. By implementing Napoleon Hill's concepts and notions, I achieved a dream that most people dismissed as idealistic at best and outright crazy at worst.

But, as I have always done, I wanted to take it one step further.

Now, I am pleased to present my own take on *Think and Grow Rich*, written specifically with the innovator and inventor in mind. This iteration of Hill's strategy is not intended so much for the accumulation of wealth, although wealth does tend to follow innovation, but as a blueprint for how to overcome the obstacles that commonly beset the inventor through the creation, patenting and marketing process. In doing this, I hope to help my own personal heroes, the people who have and implement the ideas that are shaping and changing our world, to put Napoleon Hill's strategies to work for them in an actionable, straightforward manner.

Let me reiterate that this book is intended for the inventor. It makes no distinction between race, color, creed, gender or orientation. The creator of the ubiquitous "little black dress" could as readily benefit from this book as the next Marie Curie. The heirs apparent to the throne occupied by the late Steve Jobs can find as much value in these pages as the man who invented the java sleeve. If you have an idea and the drive to develop that idea to its limits, you are the reader for whom this book was written.

*"How ridiculous and how strange to be
surprised at anything which happens in life."*

— Marcus Aurelius, *Meditations*

1

A Surprising Revelation

One morning a few weeks ago, I poured myself my first cup of coffee of the day, one of the few vices I permit myself, and settled in to read the day's news on my computer. I often peruse the financial and business world news, because as a patent attorney it's important to keep abreast of new developments and changes in both fields. As the website loaded, I tilted my head at one of the pictures that came up. The man looked familiar for some reason, but I couldn't properly place him until I saw his name.

It was a good thing I was sitting down, or I might have sloshed my coffee all over the kitchen.

The headline read, "*Med School Dropout Sells Startup for 100 Million*" and profiled one Ricardo Alexander Gomez, a former client of mine. According to the article, Mr. Gomez had just sold his company, New Wave Surgical, to an Ireland-based company, Covidien, for an amount in excess of $100 million. The company posted $21 million in revenue.

Gomez is one of my favorite success stories, because he epitomizes the spirit and drive inventors truly need to bring their innovations to the public eye.

While in medical school, Gomez noticed a rather serious problem with the cameras used during laparoscopic surgery. Surgical theaters are kept cold to reduce patient bleeding and help increase sterilization. However, this means that the tools surgeons use, including laparoscopic cameras, are cold as well. For a scalpel or similar tool, this isn't a huge problem, but when inserting a cold camera into a warm human body, the camera lens tends to fog up.

The solution to this? *A bucket of warm water.*

Gomez started working on a prototype for a self-warming surgical camera lens defogger and cleaner, pulling the fearsome study and work schedule of a medical student and developing his prototype in his rare downtime. He maxed out his credit cards to produce a working model and soon approached a surgeon with his idea. The surgeon saw the value of the prototype and agreed to help Gomez secure funding. However, the banks declined Gomez's request for a loan. The story might have ended there, but the surgeon loaned Gomez $90,000 of his own money to help Gomez jumpstart his invention, which was ultimately christened the D-HELP system.

I hadn't heard from Gomez in quite some time, so I was shocked and pleased to see that he was doing so well. His company had ranked as the fastest-growing surgical device company on *Inc.* magazine's Top 500 list and just surpassed the one-millionth procedure milestone.

This runaway success was a testament to my belief that the notion that "patents are only for big businesses" is a myth. As a patent attorney, I feel a little bit awkward sharing stories of my successful clients and basking in their reflected limelight. Yes, I got them a high quality patent but it was the client and not me that put their blood, sweat and tears into the idea and grew it into something commercially viable. In a way, I feel like an OB-GYN taking credit for "birthing" a baby that goes on to become a Nobel prize winner or a President. The OB-GYN takes just as much care and gives just as much attention to delivering the future President and

Nobel prize winning baby as he does to delivering a baby that grows up to be a homeless meth head.

Although a lot of patent attorneys have given in to the temptation to draft and file "junk" provisional patents and "fix them up" when the non-provisional application is filed, I have held our ground on only filing top quality provisional patent applications. Why? Because we never know which ideas are the ones that are going to be bought for $100 million and which ones have no potential. The only right thing to do is to protect them *all* as if they are $100 million ideas. If the provisional is not done properly at the outset, the company doing the due diligence will ignore the intellectual property and simply produce a competing device.

This quote from *Inc.* magazine's write-up on the sale really stuck hard with me, and I relate it here in its entirety.

"Perhaps the most important part of the deal was New Wave's intellectual property, as it also had several other products under development. Alex told the Journal that 'the key was to demonstrate that the patent prevented competitors from copying its product and that the law firm involved could defend it from challenges.'"

Yup. Intellectual property. Today's businesses are bought and sold not just on physical assets like land, buildings, equipment and supplies, but on the value of their ideas.

Of course, I and others in the patent law field have known this forever, but it seems that with the advent of the Internet, the notion of intellectual property being a marketable phenomenon has truly caught fire outside of the publishing industry. Software, creative work and of course tangible inventions all fall under this heading, and it's the gray area between concept and completed idea that patent law, and by extension myself, occupy.

Alex's story also had an unintended side effect on me personally. You see, I have wanted to write this book for years, but never quite managed to find the time. There was always "something." Personal and family matters, professional stresses and pressures, the demands of my clients and the students I teach as an Adjunct Professor at Nova Southeastern University Law School...if I really wanted an excuse not to write this book, most people would shrug and say, "Yeah, I think you've got quite enough on your plate."

In the same way, how many would-be inventors stand right on the edge of greatness and the kind of success Alex Gomez enjoyed and miss it because they let "something" derail them? I'm not a writer, although I did recently finish my first book, *Escaping the Gray*.

The interesting part about that book was that it was more or less universally met with shrugs and "Okay... but who cares?"

I confess that I almost let the "who cares?" sentiment derail the project altogether. After all, the story's all about me and my journey from law school to teaching and practicing patent law on my own terms. Who wants to read about that?

On the other hand, Scott Turow, a famous legal thriller writer, wrote *One L*, a book about his first year of law school. Who cares? About 30,000 law students every year who either find *One L* on their own or who are actually required by their professors to read it so they know what the first year of law school looks like and what to expect. Napoleon Hill wrote the *original Think and Grow Rich*, about the quirks and commonalities of great businessmen and innovators. Who cares? Well, considering that *Think and Grow Rich* is the undisputed number-one bestselling self-help book ever, nearly eighty years after its original publication, I think it's safe to say that a hell of a lot of people care.

In that spirit, I shrugged off the naysayers and determined to put out *Escaping the Gray*. Even if only one person read it and got something out of it, that one person would give me all the vindication I required. With *Think and Grow Rich for Inventors*, I feel confident that a lot more people are going to care about the insights I've gained and the things I've observed both in my own entrepreneurial endeavors and assisting others with theirs.

Who cares?

Well, gentle reader, obviously you do, or you wouldn't be here now. You obviously perceived a need for this book, or you wouldn't have bothered. You'd be doing something else that more directly benefits you in some way, whether it's moving your project along, solidifying your family and romantic relationships or hitting the books for whatever flavor of degree you are studying for. Whatever "something else" is, it clearly wouldn't be this. And I thank you for taking the time and giving me the chance.

Some of what you will read in these pages may not be news to you. Some of it may seem as simple and obvious as a breaking news report about water being wet. However, if you find only one thing that moves or stirs you in this book, one idea, concept or perspective that makes you see everything in a different light and finally reveals the way forward you've been seeking, then this book has value if only for that one thing. Some people may find everything in here a revelation. Others, especially those who have read *Think and Grow Rich* already, may see nothing but a retread of Napoleon Hill's ideas.

The key here is to recall that this book is designed specifically with the inventor and innovator in mind. Hill primarily targeted those with the entrepreneurial spirit, it's true, and the most successful innovators today need that entrepreneurial spirit to properly monetize and profit from their inventions. What Hill doesn't discuss in any great detail is the unique worldview of the inventor, the reason the inventor gets out of bed in the morning, the "one big idea" that is going to set the whole world on its ear.

Of course, the other factor is that innovation doesn't have to be "big" to be revolutionary. Consider the coffee cup sleeve. It's a very simple design, just a cardboard sleeve around a hot coffee cup. Did you know that silly little strip of cardboard is a patented design? It's true! There are very few places today where you can't find a coffee cup sleeve, from the local convenience store to national chains like Starbucks. Even the java sleeve inventor never expected it to be the runaway success it was, posting sales of around $8 million in its first year on the market[1]. Today, the java sleeve is all but ubiquitous anywhere you can buy hot coffee. It's a simple solution to a simple problem: hot coffee plus cup equals uncomfortably warm or even burned hands. This is why I say an invention doesn't have to change the world to be worthwhile or profitable.

Take a moment right now and look around you. What problems do you see at your desk, in your home or on your commute? Make a list. No one's grading you, so

[1] Ed Welles, 2001. "To Serve & Protect Compared" CNN *Money*. http://money.cnn.com/magazines/fsb/fsb_archive/2001/11/01/312461/

go ahead and gripe about the "small," "stupid" things. It doesn't matter what they are. All that matters is that you notice them.

Now, next to your list of problems, think of some possible solutions. Again, no one's grading you and there's not a time limit. Write them down, even if they seem absurd. A conveyor belt from the fridge to the couch so you can get a cold drink without having to risk missing an important play during the big game may not be practical, but it's a starting point. Pick one thing, the thing that really irritates you at the moment, and make that your "pain point" to solve.

This is the basis of innovation and invention: finding pain points and creating solutions for them. Mark Zuckerberg envisioned an online yearbook for people in his class. Today, he's a billionaire who keeps people around the globe connected through a little site called Facebook. At the time, he was creating a solution to a problem no one had, or at least realized they had. Nowadays, finding someone who doesn't have a Facebook account is viewed as a little odd, to say the least.

The point is that your invention doesn't have to be "big" to be a game-changer. Ultimately, what matters is coming up with a solution to a problem. If you can do this, you've already found your way to the first step in the innovation process, which we'll discuss in more detail in the next chapter.

Alex Gomez's story[2] lit a fire under me to write the book I'd always dreamed of writing since I was in law school and first discovered *Think and Grow Rich* for myself. I perceived a need for the ideas and concepts of Napoleon Hill's original work married to the mindset and worldview of the inventor-entrepreneur, a very different breed of cat than the industrialists and magnates of the early 20th century. Once I perceived the need, all that remained was to do the work, just like Alex Gomez perceived a need for the self-warming surgical camera lens cleaner and the inventor of the java sleeve perceived a need to avoid burned fingers from hot coffee cups.

What needs will you perceive? How will you solve them? Hopefully this book will serve as your road map, or at least give you some waypoints and milestones to look for.

---

[2] Brian Bandell, 2014. "The big payoff: Med school dropout sells startup for $100M" *Upstart Business Journal.* http://upstart.bizjournals.com/ entrepreneurs/hot-shots/2014/04/11/alexander-gomez-new-wave-surgical.html

*"Yes: I am a dreamer. For a dreamer
is one who can only find his way by
moonlight, and his punishment is that he
sees the dawn before the rest of the world."*

— Oscar Wilde, *The Critic as Artist*

2

The Dreamscape of the Inventor

No invention is achieved without first having a *perception of need*. This can be as simple and "silly" as not wanting to get up to change the TV channel or as elaborate and grand as developing the schematics for a colony which human beings can safely inhabit on Mars. Napoleon Hill called the first intermediary step between a dream and the finished product "desire," a single-minded, all-consuming focus on an objective. The problem with this line of thinking, which is so simple and obvious as to go largely overlooked, is that we cannot desire anything unless we first perceive a need for that thing!

Think about all the things you've ever desired in your life. It began with a "dream," or let's instead call it an "idea," because we associate the idea of "dreams" with lofty aspirations so grand that they require a Rev. Dr. Martin Luther King, Jr. to implement or with pointless, profitless woolgathering. So let's stick with the notion that "dreams" in Hill's context are herein known as "ideas."

Ideas stem from a perception of need. This is the first irrefutable bedrock principle that everyone who invents anything at all understands. Perception of need drives the search for a solution, which in turn fuels the desire to attain the solution to the need. Whether it's a better and more satisfying job, a nicer house, a spouse, a larger income or the solution to not having to stand up and manually change channels on the TV, perception of need is the first and greatest human motivator.

When I first started in patent law, I did so because there was a perception of need for the services of patent attorneys. I was hardly the first to perceive this need, but my idea had a twist: I wanted to work directly with the Fords, Edisons, Wright Brothers and Curies of our time. I wanted to guide these innovators through the often-frustrating labyrinth of patent law and help them secure the rights to their inventions from incursion by competitors, imitators and outright rip-off artists.

What was the idea?

The idea was simplicity itself: I would work with inventors.

I wanted to meet these people and draw inspiration from their struggles, setbacks and triumphs alike. I am not the inventor, but I wanted to be the friend and right hand of the inventor, at least in the legal sense. My thought process went something like, "If I can understand how the inventor gets from the perception of need to the finished product to success, perhaps I can apply the same concepts and ideas to my own work."

Of course, this wasn't codified clearly in my own mind. I had developed the "auto-suggestion" that I would work with inventors and nothing would stand in my way, but the auto-suggestion was of necessity somewhat vague and ill-defined in my own head.

This isn't to say that a bad auto-suggestion isn't better than no auto-suggestion at all. Obviously I'm where I am today and living my dream of working with inventors because of it, so the process by which I arrived at it couldn't have been all that far off the mark. Still, I sometimes wonder, if I'd taken the time to really crystalize my perception of need, if I wouldn't have arrived where I am sooner and been happier for it in the long run. Then again, there's the question of whether, if I'd gotten here sooner than I did, I would or even could be properly grateful for it.

Defining a perception of need can be as simple or complex as you care to make it. Napoleon Hill recommended setting a timeframe for achieving one's goals. This may or may not be practical, depending upon what your perception of need is. The point is to develop a simple, concrete statement of the need you perceive. "I will create a device that means I don't have to get up to change the TV channel." Hill said that you should say this in the morning and at night, upon rising and before retiring to your bed. Thus, your perception of need becomes the auto-suggestion of which I spoke earlier. I'll speak more on this, and the problems a poor auto-suggestion can cause, later.

Jay Sorensen, the man who invented the coffee sleeve in 1991, could probably sympathize with this form of auto-suggestion. After all, I'm sure that when he first looked at what he'd invented, he probably thought, "It's a cool idea, but so what? Who's going to pay money for this?"

In his first month of business, with a staff of only four, he pulled in $8 million in revenue. Today, you can't so much as set foot in a convenience store that sells coffee without seeing the java sleeve.

Like Sorensen, my auto-suggestion could have destroyed me. Fortunately, also like Sorensen, I had enough factors working in my favor that the potential negative effects of my auto-suggestion were greatly reduced. I firmly believe that anyone with a great idea hits that "wall;" that point where they look at the idea and think, "It's a cool idea...but so what?"

Once you've defined the perception of need, you've already taken the first step. Sorensen was looking for a solution to fingers burnt while holding a coffee cup. I was looking for a way to work directly with the people I knew unequivocally that I could help. The next step, then, is to develop an auto-suggestion that actually helps, instead of hinders, in creating a tangible solution to the need.

To do this, however, it is important to understand first that not every "big" invention has to be a *big invention*. It can be small and simple, but still cast a long shadow, like Sorensen's java sleeve. I'll speak more on this point later as well, because it is more relevant there than here. For now, just keep this salient point in mind for future reference.

Think for a moment about your idea. You've already defined a perception of need, or the idea would not be there. Now you need to crystallize it and reduce your perception of need to something so elementary that a child could understand it. This doesn't mean you have to spell it out chapter and verse, so to speak, but you do at least need the basics. "I will create a device that means I don't have to get up to change the channel." It's simple, direct and encapsulates precisely what you intend to do. Naturally, you'll have to change up the language to accommodate your idea, but you understand the gist.

However, a great auto-suggestion by itself is just air. You also have to have the desire to achieve your auto-suggestion. You've defined a perception of need. You've defined the auto-suggestion. Now ask yourself this: Does my auto-suggestion reflect a simple perception of need, or a real, burning desire to address that need?

You may be asking why this even matters. Defining a need is enough, isn't it?

People who create and innovate often do so at the expense of other needs and drives, in ways that others might look at as silly or downright stupid. Think back to the last time you pulled an intense creation or work session and started to feel hungry. Chances are, you did one of three things:

+ You reached for whatever snack food you had readily available.

+ You took a break and went to get something substantial in your system.

Or, most likely

+ You simply didn't eat at all, putting it off until later.

People who "forget" to eat are often ridiculed. After all, eating and sleeping are the most primal drives human beings have! Our bodies require fuel and rest, and let us know in no uncertain terms when we are beginning to surpass our design tolerance for going without. This is the sensation we describe as "hunger."

But when you simply didn't eat at all, your hunger was still present. It was merely expressing itself in a different direction: through creative output. When you got "hungry enough," you probably stopped what you were doing and gave yourself a chance to rest and replenish your resources. You had to get to the point where the hunger for food trumped any and all other considerations, likely to the point you couldn't focus on anything but your rumbling stomach! This point can be dangerous, because it's on this knife edge between creativity and physical needs that you can lose focus and inspiration.

Not long after I arrived, I was summoned to the office of one of the senior partners, Mr. Bilkerson,* by Rosetta,* my assigned secretary. We walked in together and she presented me, to which he responded with a curt nod.

"Have a seat, Rizvi," he said, aiming his slightly pudgy finger at the conference table in the center of the

* Names have been changed.

room. He was an older, imposing-looking man despite carrying a little extra weight on his frame. His voice carried even at normal conversational tones, a legacy of decades spent in the courtroom ensuring that when he spoke, everyone in the room heard him.

"Thank you, sir," I replied.

"Would you like a Krispy Kreme, Mr. Bilkerson?" Rosetta said.

"I'll take one, but I'm not going to eat it up," Bilkerson barked.

I blinked. If he wasn't going to eat it, what was he planning? To take it home for his kids? I considered this for a moment and dismissed the idea out of hand. Such a maneuver would be well beneath Bilkerson's dignity and pay grade. He could buy a Krispy Kreme franchise of his very own from his quarterly profit distribution! So what was his game?

Making matters worse, I had overslept that morning. To compensate, and I suppose as a subconscious act of atonement, I'd skipped breakfast. At the mention of the words "Krispy Kreme," I started salivating like one of Pavlov's dogs.

She didn't seem to find anything unusual or out of the ordinary about this. She hurried out and returned a minute later with a doughnut on a napkin. She didn't offer me one. Junior attorneys receive the message that they haven't yet paid their dues in all sorts of patronizing and passive-aggressive ways, and it doesn't matter if said junior attorneys have skipped breakfast and are trying to suppress rumbling stomachs or not. No treats for the kids, but the "grownups" can have all they want.

Mr. Bilkerson sat down across the table from me and began to go over the particulars of the case he wanted my assistance with. "So, here's what we've got…"

After five minutes, his voice became a drone. From there, it was only a short skip to the infamous Charlie Brown "wah-bwah-fwah-wah-fwah." I should have been paying attention and hanging on Bilkerson's every word, even though he was going a long way out of his way to be as condescending as he possibly could without giving direct offense. Every third word was "kid" this and "rookie" that, along with stern admonitions that when boiled down from lawyerese into everyday language translated to *I'll reupholster my office chair with your hide if you screw up this case.*

One reason for my inattention was my stomach, which had reacted to the presence of that doughnut like manna from heaven. I couldn't get my eyes off that silly pastry no matter how much I tried, and trying to think about anything but my empty tank worked about as well as telling someone not to think about pink elephants.

The other reason I wasn't listening as intently as I should have, and this seems really silly in retrospect, was because I was focused on the entirely bizarre exchange between Bilkerson and Rosetta over the doughnut. Why request a doughnut and then refuse to eat it? And why say "eat it up," which is the kind of clunky verbal construction most kids manage to lose by the time they're in second grade? Attorneys don't talk that way; the core of our entire profession is the elegance of language and making sure one expresses oneself precisely as intended.

In patent law, words matter even more. Every single letter of every single word has to be absolutely flawless, or it can destroy a patent application before it even sees daylight. Later in my career, I found a case where a simple typo consisting of one single letter made the difference between a unit of liquid and solid measure, invalidating the patent and leaving the company open to claims of infringement.

When it comes to patent law, *you get it right.* Period. It doesn't matter what "it" is, it has to be right.

This peculiarity is a very attractive quality to people like me, who parse words as a matter of course and are known to be anal-retentive to the point of appearing utterly inflexible. This is a perfect mindset for drafting flawless patents that will withstand judicial scrutiny. However, this quirk of mine does have its embarrassing moments too. I didn't know it at the time, but I was right in the middle of living one at that very moment.

"So!" Bilkerson clapped his beefy hands together and gave me a gimlet stare. "Do you have any questions?"

"What are you going to do with it?" I asked.

He cocked his head like a cocker spaniel hearing a strange new noise for the first time.

"With what, Rizvi?" he asked, his voice now loud enough to carry halfway through Fish & Neave's expansive office.

Yikes! He was talking about questions about the case! My heart leapt into my throat, but I didn't skip a beat.

"With the doughnut, sir. You said you weren't going to eat it—"

I trailed off as his eyes bulged and his face flushed an alarming shade of crimson. I could almost hear the gears whirring away in his head as he realized I hadn't heard the vast majority of what he said for the last twenty minutes.

"I'll *tell* you what I'm going to do!" His voice rang out like cannon fire, so loud I knew everyone in the entire building heard him. "I'm going to take this doughnut and stick it to my screen!" He picked up the doughnut and made as if to do exactly that, then set it down and gave me one of the coldest looks I'd ever received, which is saying something given the caliber of condescension I'd faced to that point.

He pressed the intercom button on his phone. "Rosetta, come in here, please."

We sat there in awful, awkward silence as we waited. Finally, she arrived and looked both of us over curiously. "Yes, Mr. Bilkerson?"

"Mr. Rizvi here seems a little peckish. Can you get some food into him?"

She raised an eyebrow. "Yes, sir. Of course. I've got a couple of takeout menus at my desk. I'll go get them."

"Hang on a second, Rosetta." He turned on me, his face as stern and impassive as the presidential busts on Mt. Rushmore. "You're excused, Rizvi. Go get some food in you and be back here at two p.m. sharp." He pointed toward the door as if imagining his index finger as a razor-sharp knife stabbing into various soft, squishy and vital bits of a smartass, newly minted attorney by the name of John Rizvi. I skulked out of his office, down the hall and back to my own office, where I sat with my head in my hands for a very long, very quiet five minutes. Maybe it was my imagination, but I could have sworn I heard Bilkerson laughing all the way back to my office.

Rosetta knocked, poked her head in, verified I was alone and came in with a number of menus for everything from deli sandwiches to takeaway Thai food. She put them in front of me and sat down.

"You okay?"

I shook my head. "I don't get what he was so upset about."

"He wasn't upset, John." Rosetta gave me a matronly smile and patted my hand. "He was just confused. You're one of the firm's Golden Boys and yet he felt you weren't paying attention. What did you say to him, anyway?"

"I asked what he was going to do with his doughnut, if he wasn't going to eat it up."

Rosetta's dark eyes went wide.

"You asked a senior partner if you could eat his doughnut?" Her tone mirrored the shock on her face.

"Well, he wasn't going to..."

Rosetta leaned back in her chair and laughed, a lot harder and louder than the observation warranted. "John, he said he didn't want to *heat* up his doughnut."

I blinked. Now her laughter made sense, maybe. "People *do* that?"

Remember I wasn't from New York and Krispy Kreme hadn't become the nationwide competition for Dunkin Donuts that it soon proved to be. Apparently it's commonplace to warm a Krispy Kreme doughnut by popping it in the microwave, as Rosetta explained. I had never heard of such thing, not growing up in Topeka, Kansas and certainly not while living in Florida.

And we certainly were not in Kansas anymore.

By the time she was done, I understood the gaffe I'd committed better than I really cared to. Even worse, I'd sabotaged myself thoroughly with one of the senior partners before I'd even managed to finish getting the Florida sand out of my shoes.

"So, what did he say after I left?" I wasn't dead certain I wanted to know, but I felt like need-to-know trumped want-to-know.

"He said he heard your stomach grumbling." She laughed. "And that it is one thing to be committed, but you have to take care of yourself and prepare for a marathon, not a sprint."

She smiled at me and waved her hand over the menus. "Now eat, get back in there and show Mr. Bilkerson that your reputation wasn't overstated."

It was good advice, and I took it. Along with a sandwich from a very good Jewish deli a couple of blocks away. But the lesson stuck hard, even though Mr. Bilkerson was never anything but nice and accommodating from that point forward and even took me under his wing and became an informal mentor of sorts at the firm. I think Rosetta had a word with him about my fears, and he did his best to allay them, even going so far as to put it around when we sent out the final billing that he couldn't have done it without me.

It wasn't the first time I'd made an error like that, and it wouldn't be the last time needless pedantry would get me in hot water. Likewise, you've probably encountered a similar situation, when you were very hungry, that distracted or completely derailed you from achieving everything you were capable of in that moment. The point of this story is to illustrate that hunger is an extremely powerful force.

You have to be just as hungry for success and for the fruition of your innovation as you are for food, if not more so! There are other primal drives that we'll address later, but for now, understand that without the raw, overriding hunger to achieve your goals, a simple statement of perception of need will not do the job. You have to desire a successful conclusion more than you desire food, sleep or sex if you really want to create something great. When this happens, your success becomes your lover, the air in your lungs, the food in your stomach and the water you drink. Everything that does not serve that singular objective is stripped away, leaving only the raw, burning desire to achieve your goal or die trying.

Chapter Takeaways

1. Identify a perception of need.

2. Create an auto-suggestion that clearly identifies the need, as well as your power to solve it.

3. Put yourself in a frame of mind where you have the burning desire to achieve your auto-suggestion and strip away anything that does not directly aid you in attaining your goals.

*"I have great faith in fools - self-confidence
my friends will call it."*

— Edgar Allan Poe, *Marginalia*

.

3

Faith in Yourself and Your Capabilities

Before I proceed, I feel that a definition of terms is necessary here.

When I say "faith," I don't necessarily mean what deity or deities, if any, you pray to or profess to worship. Religious faith is all very well and good, and many people find it an invaluable source of comfort and strength, especially when the entire world seems to have its hand set against you. What I mean when I say "faith" is the capacity to believe that you have the ability, talent and skill to create what you desire. You have faith that your idea isn't "stupid," "meaningless" or "frivolous."

And even if it is, so what? Does it satisfy a need, even one as simple as "not burning my fingers on hot coffee cups" or "keeping the kids entertained while we drive from New York to Florida?" If it satisfies a need, then it does everything it needs to do.

You recall that I talked about "auto-suggestion" in the last chapter. The auto-suggestion is the basis of faith, because it translates desire or perception of need into something real and tangible, or I might better say that it is the first step in translating the perception of need into something concrete.

When you first give an idea voice, it is at its most vulnerable, like a newborn baby. It can't defend itself and is ripe for the plucking by, say, wild dingoes. It is open to attack on any number of fronts. Some of the more common modes of attack include:

+ So what?
+ Who cares?
+ Who would want this?
+ Does this really matter?
+ Is this going to change anything?
+ This is a waste of time.
+ That thing will never fly. (Actually said to the Wright Brothers. I think we all know who got the last laugh on this one.)

The thing about faith is that you can't rely on someone else to give it to you or have it for you. Someone else can give you money, production facilities or materials. Someone else can give you work in exchange for their time, so you can focus on the business of conducting your proper work. But *no one else* can have faith for you. They may have faith *in* you, which is a very different proposition that we'll discuss further in this book. But for now, the thing you have to keep firmly in mind is that you have to have faith in yourself, for yourself.

The idea of auto-suggestion isn't a new one. It's actually almost as old as the human race. Ancient hunters started their hunts by praying to the spirits of the animals they sought for success and safety in the hunt, which is a notoriously dangerous pastime by its very nature. When the hunt was concluded, they thanked the animal spirits, or totems, for their kill. We can argue that this form of prayer was actually an auto-suggestion, creating a positive affirmation of what they needed and the assurance that they would receive it. On the other side, at the end of the hunt, they also remembered to show gratitude for what they received, in the not altogether mistaken belief that to be grateful for what they had would lead to more of the same and ingratitude and hubris would be punished by fatal accidents or illness.

Indeed, this form of auto-suggestion lies at the heart of nearly all esoteric religions and a good many occult,

New Age and philosophical movements. It may be called by different names or framed in different ways, but the end intent and result remains the same: to visualize what is desired in such a way that it makes the attainment of the object of desire or perceived need not only possible, but the *only* possible outcome! From this very simple but very powerful psychological concept of auto-suggestion comes the idea of "faith" as framed here.

However, simply reciting a slickly worded phrase isn't enough. There must be a positive emotion involved as well. Mumbling, "My invention is going to –" isn't enough if you're thinking about your maxed-out credit cards, your jerk boss who doesn't care that you have another child on the way and won't cough up that raise you need just to feed your family, that dunning letter the IRS just helpfully sent to you and seemingly everyone you've ever so much as passed on the street and so on. Saying, clearly and confidently, "My invention is going to –" is a good auto-suggestion, because you are infusing the words with positivity in your tone, in your stance, the way you hold your head, how you square your shoulders, the way every line and fiber of your body conspires to make your word Law, at least on the micro-local scale.

Think about all the people you've ever known who seem to perpetually live under a cloud. When something good happens, they wait for the other shoe to drop.

When something bad happens, they sigh resignedly and say "I knew it." This "Eeyore effect" makes many people the architects of their own downfall, because like attracts like. Money begets money. Confidence attracts confidence. An impoverished mindset attracts poverty. You've probably seen this a hundred or a thousand times in your life: the friend who can't seem to keep a job, the woman who's always bewailing why she dates an endless parade of losers, users and abusers, the person who's always complaining about how much they'd rather be somewhere that isn't where they are. All of these people have an impoverished mindset in some way, and are grimly pleased when the world lives down to their expectations. If nothing else, they can't say they're surprised.

What you want to do is the opposite of that. Instead of "faith," if that term makes you uncomfortable, say instead "belief." You have to believe that what you are doing is not only the good and right thing, it is the *only* thing and the only outcome that can be accepted. Napoleon Hill said to conduct yourself as if you already have the object of your auto-suggestion in your possession. Obviously he didn't mean to rush out to the nearest Lamborghini dealership and try to finance a $300,000 Diablo on your salary from McDonald's or Walmart. What this means is that you want to adopt the attitude that you already have it and more will come as a result, because like attracts like.

Motivational speaker Jim Rohn said, "You become the average of the five people you spend the most time around." If you spend time with criminally inclined drug addicts, it is likely that you will take on at least some of the characteristics of criminally inclined drug addicts. If you spend time with cynical types, you'll probably become cynical. If you spend time around happy, positive, upbeat people, it's likely that you'll become happy, positive and upbeat. If you spend time with successful people, you have a better chance of becoming successful.

This would be a good time to take a moment for self-reflection and evaluation. Think about the five people you spend the most time around. Now make a list of their character traits, good and bad. What are the things that attract you to them? What are the things that drive you crazy? Which of these traits are helpful to you and your dreams, and which ones are toxic? Next, think about people who embody the traits you want to emulate. What are those traits? Who are those people? How can you get into their orbit?

Please don't take this as meaning you have to completely reshuffle your circle of friends and peers! Chances are, there has been at least one time when you were hard to deal with or be around and someone stuck by you. Instead, start spending more time with Carol Confidence and less with Debbie Downer, more time with Scott Success and less time with Pete Poverty.

By doing this, you can not only start cultivating better habits for yourself, but you may just wind up lifting up your social circle at the same time!

Never underestimate the power of the subconscious mind, either. The subconscious is the part of your mind that's always running. It's where your deepest desires and fears live and grow. Your subconscious is the source of all your dreams, nightmares and sudden revelations or flashes of insight and intuition that seem to come from nowhere. Think of it as the mind's operating system, which allows the conscious mind, or desktop, to function.

The subconscious mind does not understand "No," but it understands negative emotion and energy. "I am broke" is a meaningful statement to the subconscious mind, because it works on affirmatives. "I have no money" is not a meaningful statement. "I am successful" is meaningful, while "I can't get a job" is not.

Some examples of negative statements that your subconscious refuses to process include:

- I can't
- I won't
- I don't
- I mustn't

When constructing an affirmation or auto-suggestion, it should be phrased in a positive way, so that you can really feel and act positive about it. Take a look at how we can flip the negative starts above into positive auto-suggestions.

+ *I can't get a job* becomes **I will have a job by next Friday.**

+ *I won't be successful* becomes **I am going to succeed.**

+ *I don't understand* becomes **I will learn how to do this.**

+ *I mustn't talk to that important person* becomes **This person has things to teach me that I need to learn, and I will talk to him/her.**

Now, granted, this requires not only a shift in thought, but a shift in perception. Bear in mind the subconscious understands emotion and intuition. It doesn't understand "no" as a concept, but it understands sadness, fear, hatred, jealousy and rage as well as the more positive emotions. By creating an auto-suggestion that emphasizes your capabilities in a positive way and feeding that auto-suggestion with emotions that reinforce rather than undermine it, you will find that you are able to achieve the things you want, and do so in a way that is positive not only for you, but for everyone around you as well.

I'd like to close out this chapter with another anecdote.

The note Rosetta* laid on my desk got right to the point.

Can you please come see me in my office at your earliest convenience?

I had never worked with Susan* before. We'd never co-counseled and I could count on one hand the number of times we'd even interacted in the office, outside of the weekly meetings so beloved of the corporate world and so not-so-secretly loathed by the people who have to participate in them. So why did she want to see me now, on the Monday after my return from Florida?

A miniature iceberg appeared in my stomach and began bobbing around, but one does not simply ignore a summons from one of the senior members of one's law firm if one wishes to remain a part of the practice. I had worked far too hard to get my foot in the door for any of that nonsense. Pushing my misgivings aside, I pondered the possibility that maybe she'd gotten wind of my reputation and wanted my assistance with one of her cases. It seemed like a pretty frail straw to grab onto, but I couldn't think of any other reason she'd have for requesting my presence. Scrawling my signature on the demand letter I'd just completed, I straightened my tie, took a fortifying swallow of coffee and hurried down the hall as fast as dignity and professional gravity

JOHN RIZVI, ESQ.

allowed. At her door, I rapped my knuckles twice on the hardwood and waited.

"Come in," she said.

I did so, trying to look around surreptitiously as I did so. Senior attorneys in law firms of the caliber of Fish & Neave do not ply their trade in glorified broom closets, but I still felt a wave of unadulterated envy as I looked around at the tasteful, "old guard" décor, the library of law books on the walls and the small personal touches she had employed to claim the space as her own. My office, in contrast, was half the size and not even a quarter as nicely appointed.

She looked up from her own paper-cluttered desk, her face giving away nothing.

"Have a seat, John."

"Thanks."

I did as she directed and fixed my face into a mask as expressionless as hers. The problem with having a guilty conscience is the ever-present fear that you're giving yourself away with every motion and word, but I've usually got a pretty good poker face. After a lengthy pause, the silence became unbearable.

"So, how are things?" I said.

She shuffled her papers to the side, folded her hands on the desk and looked directly at me.

"I have something to tell you that I didn't want you to know last week."

If she'd put on a penguin suit and started dancing around with a top hat and cane, I would have been less surprised. I hadn't even been in the office last week!

"Oh?"

"You may have heard that I'm retiring from Fish & Neave at the end of the year and moving to Florida." She tilted her head down and studied her hands.

I knew that already, even though her retirement hadn't been officially announced. There are few places on Earth with a more efficient grapevine than a law firm, and the wise junior attorney learns to keep an ear to the ground for the juicy tidbits of scuttlebutt on which careers can rise and fall. Her destination had been more or less secret, but I figured it as none of my business.

"Congratulations on your retirement," I said, and I meant it. Susan had a well-earned reputation as a bulldog in the courtroom, but I didn't blame her for being tired and wanting to enjoy herself for a while. What I couldn't figure was why she was telling me her intended destination. Sure, everyone in the firm knew

I had come to New York from Florida, but that didn't have anything to do with the price of oranges in Miami.

She flushed a little and an awkward silence fell. This time, having rushed into the breach once, I felt no desire to do it again. Oddly, though, this formidable woman looked somehow sheepish, like a child who'd been caught with her hand in the cookie jar. My confusion deepened. What did any of that have to do with me?

Finally, she looked up again.

"I sat the Florida bar exam last week in Tampa," said Susan. "I sat in the row behind you."

There are things one does not say aloud in a law firm because of professional standards. What goes on between one's eyeballs, however, is a very different matter.

And behind my eyeballs, a little voice started screaming "*SHIT!*" over and over again, gibbering and flailing its arms the whole while.

"*Oh,*" I said. It came out a lot less confident and more like I'd taken a hard jab in the kidney than I would have preferred.

"Um, Susan, well…why didn't you say something then?"

Another voice, this one sterner, forced the first voice to sit down and start breathing into a paper bag before turning its attention on me. *Really, John? All the things you could have said and that was the best you could do? I thought attorneys were supposed to be smart!*

The voice had a point, but I ignored it and instead worked on regaining my professional composure.

Susan smiled a little. "Because I didn't want you to be nervous and thinking about me or Fish & Neave through the exam. I figured I would wait until the test was over and then say hello but you left right away."

She paused for a beat, as if trying to find the right thing to say, and then continued. "Just so you know, I have not told anyone at the law firm that I saw you taking the Florida bar exam and I will keep this between us. I just would feel very awkward having seen you there and not mentioning anything."

Confession is good for the soul, and since she'd broken the ice, I didn't see any point in dancing around it. "Susan, can I tell you something?"

Now she turned the full wattage of her smile on me. "Of course. Everything is off the record."

This may not seem like much of a concession, but "off the record" between attorneys means something very different than it does among civilians. It meant she was offering me the same confidentiality and privilege that attorneys offer clients, and that I had no need to keep secrets.

Feeling as if I was plunging from a great height into ice water, I took a deep breath and said, "I want to go out on my own and form my own law firm." She raised her eyebrows and I hurried on. "I'm tired of doing corporate patent work. I want to help young start-up companies and individual inventors."

Susan smirked. "There are inventors in Florida?"

Way to go for the cheap shot, Susan, I thought, and then immediately corrected myself. Lifelong New Yorkers think civilization ends at the Hudson River and doesn't pick up again properly until L.A. More to the point, the Florida "hanging chad" debacle in the 2000 Presidential race was still fresh in everyone's minds. I'd taken enough guff and razzing about it to build up a thick skin, but the New York state of mind still irked me sometimes.

"Yes, there are," I assured her.

"Maybe they can invent a ballot machine that actually works. Hey, you could get in the history books just for that!"

I laughed along with her, but somewhere in the back of my mind, I felt a cold determination that somehow, some way, the last laugh would belong to me. Her casual New York condescension had just sealed my fate.

I had my auto-suggestion. I had my faith.

And nothing, and no one, was going to stand in my way.

Chapter Takeaways

1. Evaluate your frame of mind and refine it to accept positivity rather than negativity.

2. Craft your auto-suggestion in such a way that it gives your subconscious permission to seek out the desired outcome.

3. Surround yourself with people who exemplify the traits you wish to attract into your life, rather than those who do not.

*"Any fool can know. The point
is to understand."*

— Albert Einstein

4

Developing Specialized Knowledge

There is an ongoing idea that entrepreneurs have to be generalists to survive in today's world. That is, they have to know a lot about a number of different topics in order to be successful. A quick review of well-known innovators shows that this isn't at all the case.

Henry Ford famously sued a newspaper for libel over a scathing editorial in which he was accused of being ignorant. During the trial, the attorney for the newspaper decided to demonstrate just how ignorant Ford was by asking him questions about American history which most schoolchildren, then and now, would know. Ford's most often repeated answer was "I don't know." One particularly brilliant reply was this one, to the question, "How many soldiers did the British Army send over to America to put down the rebellion of 1776?" Ford's reply: "I'm not sure of the exact number of soldiers the British sent over, but I have heard it was a considerably greater number than ever went back."

Finally, losing patience with the whole business and seeing which way the wind was blowing, Ford said, "If I should really *want* to answer the foolish question you have just asked, or any of the other questions you have been asking me, let me remind you that I have a row of electric push-buttons on my desk, and by pushing the right button, I can summon to my aid men who can answer *any* question I desire to ask concerning the business to which I am devoting most of my efforts. Now, will you kindly tell me, *why* I should clutter up my mind with general knowledge, for the purpose of being able to answer questions, when I have men around me who can supply any knowledge I require?"[3]

Ford's terse and on-point answer turned the tide of the trial to his favor, and moreover set a model that today's innovators and businessmen would be wise to adopt. Instead of trying to become an expert in every field

[3] As recounted by Hill in *Think and Grow Rich* (1937)

relevant to a given innovation, whether it's software or socks, the wise inventor focuses on developing the specialized knowledge most relevant to building a product that works.

Today, too many people think they have to be accountants, lawyers, MBAs, human resources liaisons, project managers and so on in addition to doing the thing they're trying to focus on. This is a dangerous mistake because it draws time and energy away from the process of invention, refinement and development in order to deal with matters which could be more effectively attended to by people with the requisite specialist knowledge in their own right. What often happens is, instead of a smoothly functioning company built around a great product, the product suffers because the innovator is spending too much time and effort learning about ancillary topics "on the fly," placing the inventor and their creation at risk of any number of legal and marketplace horrors.

It is far better and more effective to learn to source and purchase the specialized knowledge a business requires. With the freelance and gig economy employing between 16%-30% of the US workforce in a full-time or part-time capacity,[4] outsourcing specialist knowledge is literally a matter of a few mouse clicks, keystrokes

---

[4] Sources vary on this because the way freelance labor is defined and categorized changes depending upon the underlying intent and purpose of the individual survey.

and entering a credit card number. Of course, vetting freelancers to make sure they have the skills they claim to is another matter, but you'd be doing the same thing if you were considering a candidate for a full-time position with the company, wouldn't you? The advantage of freelancers is that you aren't required to deal with payroll taxes, insurance benefits or 401(k)s, so while you may pay a higher hourly or per-project rate, you ultimately benefit by having specialist knowledge readily available for a cheaper price than the cost of onboarding, training and supplying benefits to a regular full-time employee whose specialist skills may not be needed every single day.

At this stage, you already have your idea, you have your auto-suggestion and you have your faith or belief in the soundness and value of your idea, which is reinforced by the auto-suggestion. Since you have the idea, the next step is to evaluate your level of knowledge and determine what specialist knowledge or skills you will need to bring your invention from the theoretical into actual being.

For a software programmer, this may mean learning a new coding style or using existing code in a new way. Someone designing a new type of sock may need to analyze different means of tailoring or producing socks to make the product more durable, colorfast, comfortable or all of the above. The possibilities are limitless, but only by delving into the particulars of a specific industry can you expect to develop the specialized knowledge you need and more importantly, find out both what you don't know but know you don't know and what you don't know and don't know you don't know!

One of my favorite stories in this vein is about a client of mine named Troy Faletra. Troy is a veteran sailor and water sportsman who invented something that I believed in the first time I saw it. I first met Troy some years after the incident that would make him his fortune…and nearly cost him his life.

Troy came to my office one afternoon for a consultation about patenting his invention. When I met him in the conference room, we went through the usual pleasantries and preliminaries and then he said, "I have the prototype with me. Would you like to see it?"

"Of course!" I promptly replied.

Troy produced this funny-looking olive drab package, about the size of a lunchbox. It had a cord on one side. He set the package on the table, looked at me and with perfect seriousness, said, "You may want to step back."

This made me raise an eyebrow, but I bowed to the superior knowledge of the guy who built the thing and did as he directed. He gave the cord a sharp tug and jumped back.

It only took a second to understand why.

When Troy pulled the cord, it activated a CO_2 cartridge that began to inflate the raft. And I watched the raft get bigger…and bigger…and BIGGER, until I was honestly worried that the raft would be too big for the relatively small conference room! To my relief, the raft stopped inflating well short of disaster, at its final length dimension of about eight feet. The demo had done its job and impressed the hell out of me, but even more telling and exciting was the look on Troy's face as the raft deployed.

He looked like he'd just witnessed the birth of his child. And in a way, I suppose that was exactly true. This raft was the end result of his hard work, determination and creativity, and even though I'm more or less a landlubber, I immediately recognized the potential. More importantly, I recognized the creative passion and inspiration that had made me want to work with inventors in the first place. It was a watershed moment for me, because I knew then and there that all the hard work I'd put in to get where I was had been totally worth it just to see that awed, joyous look on Troy's face.

"How did you come up with that?" I asked, once we collapsed the raft and returned to our seats.

He looked me right in the eye, his face perfectly deadpan, and said, "My boat sank."

Something about the way he said it set every hair on my body standing at attention. It reminded me of the way a war veteran deflects questions by answering them in the simplest and most direct way possible. Three simple words, and I knew I had to hear the whole story. Because I think somewhere deep down, I knew that it would haunt me to my dying day if I didn't.

"What happened?" I pressed.

He thought for a moment. Then he spoke.

"I sank in my boat about nine miles off shore and I radioed for help. I gave out a mayday name, gave my coordinates to the United States Coast Guard and once my boat started to sinking, within five minutes it was about thirty feet below my feet. Being a stubborn man, I decided that it would be better for me to swim instead of hold my position and wait for them to come rescue me.

"So what I decided to do was swim to shore. Well, that ended up taking close to sixteen hours and once I got to shore, it was definitely a great moment, but it wasn't until several years later after other people's incidents and their stores and – you know, that was when I thought and decided that there should be a need for alternative regulated products on vessels in the United States and worldwide and that's where it all started."

I listened to his story, enthralled. Despite his calm delivery, something about the way he told it or the look in his eyes made me actually feel the water around me, the fear of being so far from shore and knowing rescue was uncertain at best. The muscles in my arms cramped in sympathy at the thought of swimming for a grueling sixteen hours straight to get back to land, all the way never knowing what hazards might be making their way up from the ocean floor. This guy had what one of my Jewish colleagues at Fish & Neave had called "chutzpah."

I wondered if I could have done what he did in the same position. Even to this day, I still do when I think about this story. Truthfully, part of me kind of doubts it.

"I think I can help," I told him. "What brought you to me?"

It turned out a number of factors had influenced him. He had seen one of those "$200 patent" commercials on TV and it got him to wondering just how secure and legitimate a patent acquired that way actually would be. (Spoiler alert: It's not. At the absolute best, they're a starting point. At worst, companies like that are outright scams.) Thankfully, Troy wasn't taken in by the hype. Instead, he did his homework and found me.

"What really swung it for me was the fact you teach at Nova Southeastern."

"Oh?" I said, raising both eyebrows.

"Yeah. I wanted to work with someone local and who knew their stuff. I figure anyone who teaches patent law classes has the chops to do it right."

At the risk of blowing my own horn, I had to concede the validity of his point.

Ten years after that initial meeting, ThrowRaft.com features the first throwable, inflatable raft approved by the US Coast Guard for use in all vessels. This is the nautical equivalent of having a drug approved by the FDA, because of the USCG's stringent requirements for personal flotation devices. The TD2401, the final version of Troy's original design, replaces both ring buoys and square cushions without violating Coast Guard personal watercraft regulations.

After we got his patent locked down, we needed to get him a trademark for the ThrowRaft. I was glad to help, because between the inventor's fever in his eyes and the brilliant simplicity of the design, I knew he was on to something huge.

To my immense pleasure, time proved me right. I've served as his counsel on a number of other business-related whosits and whatsits since that first meeting. ThrowRaft.com is a thriving business and Troy continues to spend the bulk of his time when he's not running the company out on the water, surfing or serving as a yacht captain.

Out of the hundreds of inventors I have helped over the years, a few went on to become magnificently wealthy. Many others were able to retire and get out of the 9-to-5 rut with the income from their patents. All of them have inspired me in some very real, very tangible way. But when I think about why I do what I do, Troy's story is one of the ones that always comes back to me. It was a surprising and inspiring experience, and it's the kind of story that reminds me why I do what I do on the days when my passion starts to feel like just another day at the office.

I know someone is going to say something about client-attorney privilege. For the record, I have Troy's full consent, permission and authorization to relate his story here. I'm very pleased for that, because it's a great story and I'm proud to have played a part in it.

Troy had a great deal of specialist knowledge about ocean survival and safety, maritime regulations and boating in general. What he learned about manufacturing he learned only to the degree absolutely necessary to develop a working prototype. I assume an accountant handles his day-to-day bookkeeping, and I know for a fact that he doesn't do his own legal work. (I have filled that role for him in the past.) By not cluttering his head up trying to become an expert in areas that were irrelevant to the actual invention and recruiting people with the specialized knowledge he needed, when he needed it, he was able to make ThrowRaft a going concern.

Troy's story is a great one because he had an idea. Somehow, some way, he created an auto-suggestion that permitted him to see the idea through. He had faith in the validity of his idea and its potential to save lives. He also had the specialist knowledge he required to develop a prototype that would make his point and attract others who could also see the value and potential of the ThrowRaft concept. But, in addition to these qualities, which we've already discussed at some length, he had the imagination to see not only what the state of affairs was with regards to life rafts…but what it *could* be.

We will discuss imagination more in the next chapter, but for now, keep in mind that we are fortunate to have Google and the broader Internet right at our fingertips. We can find information in a few seconds that used to be the work of hours to locate, isolate and pinpoint, shuttling books back and forth from shelf to table and back again only to often walk away, dejected and defeated because that *one key piece* of information eluded us. Today, you can find full tutorials on how to program in HTML, CSS and JavaScript, free for the cost of clicking a mouse button and your monthly Internet subscription. Just about any piece of information, no matter how esoteric, can be found on the Web if you're willing to look hard enough.

However, while this method of getting information can be useful for a one-off need, such as "Why the **** isn't this ******* code doing what I need it to do?" it may not be the greatest for finding and more importantly, understanding the complexities of tax law, for example. For this, a specialist who has taken the time and effort to achieve an expert (or at least higher than your own) understanding of the subject matter is a better investment in terms of time, money, resources and probable outcome. Be the specialist you need to be for your innovation to take off, and let the other specialists do their jobs in turn.

Henry Ford made a great point in court; one that still holds true today. If you have the specialized knowledge you need for the overarching task at hand, you can always recruit or contact other specialists for the peripherals. Remember, multitasking means you're doing a lot of things, and probably few, if any, of them well.

Chapter Takeaways

1. Focus on developing the specialist knowledge you need to effectively develop your innovation.

2. Outsource, crowdsource or hire specialist knowledge on an employee or freelance basis as needed.

3. Don't try to become an expert in "all the things." Focus on the areas that most directly pertain to what you're trying to accomplish.

"Imagination will often carry us to worlds that never were, but without it we go nowhere."

— Carl Sagan

5

Imagination and Developing Potential

In the realm of patent law, "scope" and "limits" are often discussed, especially in the earlier stages of launching a patent. "Scope" means how far the patent can be extended and what uses, functions or purposes it covers. The point at which the scope ends is the "limit." A patent that tries for too wide of a scope is just as problematic as a patent that only covers a single application of the invention.

In one case, the patent will be denied because, for example, you cannot patent the process of using a word processing program to create a book. You can patent a specific word processing program that does something unusual or unique, but you can't try to patent what already exists.

In the second case, the patent will be granted, but if the patent language is too limited, competitors will apprehend other possible applications and move right around the limits of the original patent to increase the scope of their own knock-off designs. This leaves the inventor's design more vulnerable and makes it less likely that the inventor can recover damages arising from what is ethically and morally patent infringement but legally not. One important thing to remember is that there is no "spirit of the law." Only the "letter of the law" matters.

The importance of imagination here becomes obvious. It's not only what the innovation *can* do that matters, but what it *could* do. It takes both imagination and creativity to look beyond the usual applications of, say, a crescent wrench and envision different ways in which it could be employed that were never intended by its inventor. While it's vanishingly unlikely that at this point one could patent a usage for the crescent wrench that hasn't already been conceived of, it nevertheless serves as a useful intellectual exercise for considering how other innovations might be expanded beyond their original usages and thus increase their scope.

Knowledge, imagination and creativity are inextricably linked. From knowledge flows the capacity to not only understand what exists but perceive the need for something new or different. However, perception of need by itself is not sufficient. There must also be the imagination to envision the solution to the need and the creativity to implement the solution, which is also a function of knowledge.

Because of this, we can say that imagination does not exist in a vacuum, but rather as a continuum. The continuum of imagination runs as follows:

We start with *imagination* to obtain perception of need.

We amass knowledge to identify the perception of need.

We mix imagination with knowledge to identify feasible solutions to the perception of need. This is important because a magic wand is useless to the inventor, cool as it would be to have one that just does things and makes them work. We need real, actionable, replicable and scalable solutions.

We mix creativity with imagination and knowledge to develop a functional prototype and bring the imaginary into the realm of the factual. A good example of this is the modern tablet. This technology first hit the TV screens and imaginations of Americans with the original *Star Trek* TV series. Today, a lot of modern computing technology owes a debt to inspiration from the series writers' imaginations.

Technology that was seen in 1967 to be 300+ years in the future from the viewers of *Star Trek* are today so commonplace that someone who doesn't have a smart phone, laptop or tablet is viewed almost as an object of pity in modern society. Some believe it is not a coincidence that Apple's iPad bears a striking resemblance to the *Star Trek* datapadd in terms of both form and function.

Thus, imagination is both the beginning and end of the creative cycle, from the inception of the idea to developing the functional prototype.

This is a good time to reiterate a theme which I will be returning to often throughout the course of this book: There is no such thing as "too small" an innovation! The java sleeve wasn't "big," "sexy" or "revolutionary" in itself. At its most basic level, it's just a strip of cardboard. It was the way in which that strip of cardboard was used that makes the difference. The inventor of the java sleeve didn't invent corrugated cardboard, coffee or coffee cups…and yet his invention is evident just about anywhere a person buys coffee today. But what the inventor of the java sleeve did bring to the table was a unique way of looking at the problem and finding a solution that required nothing more than the application of one small extra step in the process of creating a cup of coffee. In short, he applied imagination to a problem, found a solution...and became quite wealthy in doing so.

One example of this that stands out in my mind happened not long after I married my wife, Saba. Shortly after our wedding, we went on a trip to Florida to visit my family. One day, we took the day to pursue our own interests and play tourist. We wandered the beach, explored the shops and bought ice cream. While we ambled along, pointing out interesting things to each other and talking about everything and nothing, one of the problematic flaws in the human machine caught up with me.

I located a restroom and walked inside, only to realize that I should have asked Saba to set down one of her bags and hold my ice cream cone until I got back. It was the waffle kind with the pointy tip, and using the bathroom one-handed is a difficult business at best. Looking around, I quickly spotted a possible solution.

Taking a mostly empty roll of toilet paper from one of the stalls, I stuck the cone down inside it and put it on the counter. To my satisfaction, it stayed upright. I finished my business, put a fresh roll in the stall whose roll I'd liberated for my own nefarious purposes, washed my hands and sauntered outside, with the ice cream cone still in the denuded toilet paper roll.

We walked leisurely along for a while, completely unaware that anything was amiss. Sometime later, Saba glanced at my cone as I lifted my hand to point at something nearby. She did a perfectly comical cartoon double-take.

"Um."

"Yes?"

"What's that on your ice cream cone?" She peered closer. "Is that a *toilet paper roll?*"

I shook my head and smiled. "No," I told her proudly. "I just invented an ice cream cone holder!"

"While you were in the bathroom." Her perfectly flat tone told me she wasn't fooled.

"Yes."

She smiled and rolled her eyes, pecked me on the cheek and took my hand in a way that set my nerdy, creative, anal-retentive heart pitter-pattering in a way that scared and intoxicated me at the same time.

This story seems ridiculous at first glance. No, I never did patent my "ice cream cone holder." Looking back, I probably could have and maybe even should have. At the time I did it, though, I wasn't thinking in terms of whether I'd invented something. I just needed to use the bathroom and not have to worry about my ice cream at the same time, and when I espied a possible solution, I took advantage of it. It took some imagination, but I made the same mistake I now caution inventors about on a nearly daily basis: the error of assuming the idea wasn't "big enough" to be worth pursuing to a possibly profitable conclusion. As it stands now, I plead youth and being a newlywed, which, as anyone who's been in either or both positions will understand, tends to cloud one's judgment.

However, this incident showed me that even the most seemingly ludicrous "invention" can be useful, and that necessity truly is the mother of invention. I had perceived a need and found a solution for that need almost immediately. Because of this, my "invention" cast a long shadow over my life by demonstrating that solutions are where you find them and that there is no such thing as a solution that's "too small." This helped give rise to another auto-suggestion, one that was more positive: "I will have my own firm and help inventors directly."

Imagination can also work against you and your auto-suggestion, though. The key is to keep imagination directed to the places where it helps you and your process instead of hindering it. When imagination runs wild in unprofitable directions, it can be disastrous. When I lived in New York City and worked for the patent law firm of Fish & Neave, I inadvertently developed a poor auto-suggestion because of my imagination and one singular event that changed everything for me.

When I was in New York City, my office was right across the street from Radio City Music Hall in Mid-town Manhattan. There were more people in the building that I worked in than there were in many entire cities in Florida. Add to that the building across the street and the building diagonal to us and the building next to that and pretty soon you are talking about a significant population within just the confines of one block. Factor in the buildings on the adjacent blocks and the numbers became daunting indeed.

Anytime you have that many people, statistically you run the chance of people needing emergency services sooner or later. I remember one distinct occasion when I saw someone being carried out in a stretcher as I arrived at my building one morning.

"What happened?" I asked in wide-eyed amazement as the crowd gathered around the ambulance.

"One of the insurance executives at XYX Insurance had a heart attack at his desk," a man standing nearby answered. His manner was almost matter-of-fact, tainted only with a minor stain of annoyance at the delay in getting to his office rather than concern for the other person.

"Oh my God!" I exclaimed, unable to understand how someone could be so calm and blasé about death.

It seemed like such a normal occurrence to the gentleman that explained what happened, but when he saw my surprise, he explained. "It happens three or four times a year around here. Someone will just drop dead at their desk," he said, with typical New York sangfroid.

An eye-opening experience for a young associate and a strong reminder to me that all of us have a limited amount of time here and when that time is up….it is up.

I didn't really know what an "insurance executive" was or did but it seemed to me to represent the "gray twilight" that Theodore Roosevelt spoke about in this quote:

Far better it is to dare mighty things, to win glorious triumphs even though checkered by failure, than to rank with those timid spirits who neither enjoy nor suffer much because they live in the gray twilight that knows neither victory nor defeat.

So this insurance executive went to work day after day after day…and one day just *died*. All his hopes. All his dreams. All his ambitions. Everything gone with him to his grave.

After that day, every time I would head into work, I would subconsciously think about the ambulance and be reminded about the "gray twilight."

Day after day, I went to my desk and toiled through my day, dreaming of leaving the legal factory behind and starting out on my own. Representing individual inventors and start-ups. Helping people live their dreams by quitting the corporate rat race and pursuing their passions.

Every day, I thought about the "gray twilight that knows neither victory nor defeat."

It dawned on me that I was living in the gray twilight. I was comfortable and making incredible money but I was slowly withering away. I felt myself suffocating because I knew neither victory nor defeat. I had a wife and newborn daughter depending on me to do the "right" thing for my family…but I was terrified to acknowledge that I didn't know what the "right" thing was.

This became an auto-suggestion of mine. *What am I doing?*

I would visualize an ambulance as I came into work and visualize one as I left. *I need to get out of the gray twilight,* I would think each time I passed the spot where I saw the ambulance.

I became keenly aware of ambulances, the way one becomes aware of particular brands of cars when they are in the market for or have just purchased a new car. For example, if you are thinking of buying a Honda Accord, you will see them everywhere. They were always there, but now there's a feeling of kinship, of belonging to that club, and the Fords and Chevys and BMWs all fade into the background. Instead of registering on your subconscious, the car you want or own is now top-of-mind.

In much the same way, my consciousness focused upon ambulances in the city. I walked to work from my apartment in Mid-town, and every time I would see an ambulance I would think of the poor soul that lived his life timidly and knew neither victory nor defeat.

The problem with this auto-suggestion was that it didn't define a goal, a timeframe or measures by which I intended to attain a goal. It was the kind of auto-suggestion that Hill refutes on the grounds of being self-defeating, self-denying and self-deprecating. It wasn't framed in the language of inspiration or desire, but rather that of fear.

My partner, Glenn Gold, was one of my best law school friends and we had often discussed opening up our own law firm. Once we both decided to leave we would exchange emails encouraging each other to resign. Glenn was a patent attorney at Motorola at the time. He would encourage me and I would encourage him...but both of us were scared to death of leaving our cushy jobs and nothing would happen.

Somewhere in the middle of this, I started to become very aware of the passage of time. My daughter was growing so fast that she almost seemed like a different person from morning, when I left, to night, when I returned. She became a sort of symbol, a metaphor for the rushing hands of the clock, shearing away seconds and minutes, whittling away hours and days from my life. In this instance, my anal-retentive nature worked against me, because I've always been very analytical. However, my analysis turned to paralysis as I registered every ambulance that passed by and realized that soon the clock hands could turn into the Grim Reaper's scythe. This frightening progression redoubled as Saba gave birth to our second daughter in mid-2001.

I began to document my internal struggle in writing a weekly email to my family. I am one of four children and am very close to my two younger sisters. I would send a weekly email to them and my parents on the progress of starting my own firm. Week after week I would give a synopsis of the steps I had taken and document my emotions as I prepared to resign. I felt like I was jumping off a cliff. Newly married and with two young daughters, I was struggling with the decision of leaving a wonderful and prestigious law firm with health insurance, a partnership track and stability to go out on my own. I had no clients, no idea how or where I would get clients, no revenue, no staff, no office, no idea of how we would survive without any reliable income source and to leave on the basis of nothing more than a dream that I shared with Glenn.

Glenn also had the enviable position of being an in-house patent attorney at Motorola and was hesitant to pull the trigger as well, for much the same reasons. So we dreamed lots, and did nothing.

The weekly emails continued for a year, then two years, then three years. My family was supportive but I think they were convinced that I was "all talk" and that I would never have the courage to launch my own firm.

One day my sister forwarded an email to me from a perfect stranger. I had inadvertently set up a group email with the domain of my father's email address wrong and for three years the emails were going to an outsider. He had been reading my weekly emails, complete with my most intimate thoughts, fears and worries, for three years and had had enough. I don't blame him for that.

Now, my father was relatively new to email and his email address was one my much younger brother (who was fifteen at the time) got for him. He took our last name, *Rizvi*, and added a "CK" at the end for Calvin Klein so my dad would supposedly have a "hip" email. Unfortunately, my dad didn't know the "CK" stood for

"Calvin Klein" and used to refer to his email which was RizviCK as <u>RizVick@hotmail.com</u>. Except that it was <u>RizVick@yahoo.com</u>. Little did I know, there was a <u>Rizvick@hotmail.com</u>.

And I heard from him.

From the tone of his email, he had written many times before asking me to please stop emailing him. I didn't get any of the emails as I guess my spam filter caught them, but on this final missive to me he copied everyone. My parents, my sisters and me all got this email. And it was *brutal*.

The language was obscene and vulgar. I would have to "bleep" out every other word to reprint it here, but the gist was, he was beyond sick and tired of my inadvertent insistence on dragging him into my struggles. Vulgarity aside, what he said hit home with the force of a baseball bat to the stomach.

Face it. You will never have your own firm. You talk about it and dream about it but you don't have the balls to follow through. Losers like you are made to spend their entire lives working for someone else and building someone else's company. You are made to be miserable because you are stuck in that horrible middle ground where you have neither the courage to follow your dreams nor the intelligence to know to give them up.

This was in the middle of June, 2001. I read the email, once angrily, again thoughtfully, and the last time with a feeling of slow-burning determination.

My imagination was working against me, shackling me in place with chains of fear and self-doubt, keeping me exactly where I was. I wasn't growing or developing. I wasn't doing anything new or innovative, nor was I so much as a single step closer to my stated goal than I'd started.

It was time to start channeling my imagination to the positive, not the negative. I needed to permit myself to succeed instead of allowing myself to fail.

In much the same way, the inventor needs to learn to target and direct imagination and energy to serving the intended purpose of the auto-suggestion, not undermining it. This is not easy to do, and I don't mean to imply that it is. It requires constant discipline, focus and self-awareness. Anything that takes away from the prerequisites of the auto-suggestion, any imagined fear or concern that erodes confidence or the ability to see the way forward, should be treated as an implacable enemy and dealt with just as ruthlessly.

Imagination can be your best friend and ally, or your greatest foe. Which it will prove to be is largely up to you.

Chapter Takeaways

1. Know where you are on the continuum of imagination, whether you're just starting or one step from the finished prototype.

2. Keep in mind that there is no such thing as an innovation that's "too small."

3. Let your imagination guide your efforts, not hinder them.

4. Your imagination should serve your auto-suggestion, not the other way around.

"Without leaps of imagination or dreaming,
we lose the excitement of possibilities.
Dreaming, after all is a form of planning."

— Gloria Steinem

6

Organized Planning as a Function of Imagination

If you've read this far and have been implementing the steps we've discussed, you're already well on your way to achieving an organized plan. Think of this plan as your blueprint for success, a roadmap, if you will, to where you want to be. It's not enough to say, "I'm going to create an ice cream cone holder!" Even if you do so, you may not have the specialist knowledge you need to keep and maintain account ledgers, hire people, market your invention, patent the idea or any number of other necessary but often-overlooked minutiae. This is where organized planning comes into play.

The basis of organized planning is to surround yourself with a group of people who can help you on your way and to whose spheres you add value as well. Walking into a group of people with your hand out and asking for help places you in a vulnerable position, less than half a step above a beggar. This is to be avoided if at all possible, because the more of this you have to do, the less likely it is that you will be viewed as a desirable partner, and it is as a partner that you are most likely to be able to add value.

Because of this, the first order of business is to determine what, besides your invention, you bring to the table. There is an old saying that "Ideas are worthless," and this is true…to a point. It is more accurate to say that "Unsupported ideas are worthless." If you have a prototype, you have a supported idea and a thing of value. This book started as an idea, value zero. The fact that you are reading it now and have come this far with it makes it a supported idea with a relative value to you of whatever you receive from it.

This observation requires a detour, because I want to discuss the notion of value in a more detailed way. Knowing your value and the value of what you have to offer is one of the most important and most frightening things that will ever happen to you in your life, because when you realize what you are really worth, the thought of settling for less will anger and disgust you. It is a very powerful moment and it will redefine the rest of your life, for better or worse, from that point forward.

Robert A. Heinlein posited an example of value in his novel *Starship Troopers*. The example involved three cooks of relative skill levels from incompetent to expert, all trying to make an apple tart from identical ingredients. The incompetent chef transformed the ingredients into an inedible mess with no value. The competent chef made a competent tart of modest value. However, the expert chef made a delicious tart of high value with no more effort than the competent chef expended in making a merely competent pastry.

We all have points of expertise, points of mere competence and points where we are completely incompetent. These points will vary from person to person depending upon what is being called into question. In the realm of patent law, I can say in all immodesty that I am probably one of the best based upon my track record. When it comes to software, I'm competent enough to be able to follow and understand what is being presented to me to patent, but it's even money whether or not I would be able to replicate it on my own. But when we're discussing accounting and managing billing, I'm hopeless and will be the first to admit it. For this, I engage an expert rather than try to do it myself with potentially disastrous results.

This type of brutally honest self-evaluation is the first step in organized planning. It's not enough to know what you know and what you don't know, which is a philosophical wormhole at the best of times anyway. You know what you know and you may have an idea of what you don't know, but what you don't know you don't know is always the devil in the details. For this reason, if you're not absolutely certain of what you know, you're better off acting like you know nothing at all. The point is that it is what you know that someone else does *not* know that will establish your value within the circle of people you need to amass.

Think back to Henry Ford. He wasn't a stupid man by any means. We can argue that he was ignorant of basic knowledge that most people take for granted, but by his own admission, he saw such knowledge as nothing more than trivia and surrounded himself with people who possessed the knowledge he didn't see the need to amass. In this way, he freed himself to develop the knowledge that most directly related to his business and overriding interests while at the same time providing value to others who possessed more specialized knowledge of things that were not directly related to the business in the form of employment. His value lay in his specialized knowledge and his ability to harness the knowledge of others to produce a concrete, tangible result.

Because of this, you should focus on the specialist knowledge you bring to the table. Troy Faletra brought a high degree of knowledge of seamanship and Coast Guard regulations to his invention. The inventor of the java sleeve developed a single product and created a fortune from it.

Another thing to keep in mind is that value is largely a matter of perception. Water to a man dying of thirst in the desert is more valuable than anything except his own life. To someone drowning in a lake, water is worthless and a source of trouble to boot. Thus, if your background is in software, it makes little sense to approach other people with a software background unless you and they can fill in knowledge gaps to create a final, functional product. If you know software and another person knows marketing and a third person knows accounting, you now have something to trade because the perception of value will, by definition, be greater.

Napoleon Hill espouses the notion of the Master Mind, or a group of people who complement and cover each other's strengths and weaknesses. No single person knows everything there is to know, nor can one person amass a working business model. This may work fine for a little while, but ultimately specialists will need to be sought out, recruited and brought on board to develop an idea from drawing board to dining room table to a legitimate business enterprise. Development of a Master Mind can help speed up this process by overcoming roadblocks caused by lack of knowledge or skill in more mundane but nevertheless crucial areas. A board of directors or the C-suite of a modern business are good examples of a Master Mind.

The trouble with this is that in developing a Master Mind, some control over the invention and direction of the company must be sacrificed by the innovator to the others who have put "skin in the game." This is not altogether a bad thing, but it can be very frightening to an inventor who suddenly sees the fruits of their labor taken from them and applied in ways they never intended or desired. For this reason, not only should the individual members of the Master Mind complement each other in terms of abilities and points of weakness, but the Master Mind should be comprised of a group of people who see the same results, potential and metrics as desirable outcomes. This will help reduce friction and ensure everyone involved is working toward a common goal, rather than their own self-interests.

When I first began to consider breaking away from Fish & Neave to start my own practice, my Master Mind consisted of my friend and future partner, Glenn Gold; my mother, father and family; and my wife, Saba. I've already related the trigger that started me looking around at my life, seeing it as more of a gilded cage than the aircraft I needed to fly me to the point I ultimately wished to attain. Now let me show you how it became personal, and how an unintended addition to my Master Mind finally gave me the impetus to move forward with the plan.

You recall I spoke earlier about the embarrassing email gaffe that resulted in a complete stranger reading my most intimate thoughts and fears vis a vis starting my own firm. From somewhere in the Blue Nowhere, this stranger, whom I'd never met face-to-face and likely never will, reached out and gave me a hard virtual slap across the face. At the time I didn't appreciate it, but this outsider's perspective on the situation made the final dominos fall into place.

Because he was right. I was planning and plotting and scheming my life away…and getting not one millimeter closer to my goal. Plans are fine and good things in their place, but they are not a substitute for action! This stranger taught me that you can have all the planning in the world, but without the guts (or whatever body part you care to insert in place of "guts"), you're never going to get anywhere. I'm fairly certain that after years of hearing about my plans and seeing me stay right where I was, planning be damned, even my closest confidantes had just about written my plans off as nothing more than frustrated venting.

To be perfectly honest, before that email, I had too.

The point here is that no plan ever gets anywhere if you don't implement it. The unintended addition to my Master Mind of that one person who had the audacity to call me out on my lack of forward motion proved to be the catalyst that got me moving. It wasn't the plan that was the problem, it was my own fear of implementing it that held me back.

So what does an organized plan look like?

An organized plan is:

- **Actionable:** You can implement your plan quickly and effectively.

- **Flexible:** You can make adjustments as needed. This point is particularly crucial, because committing to a plan without building in adjustment phases where needed is nothing more than stubbornness. It's not a plan if you're just bulling blindly through it.

- **Aware of potential problems:** There is an old saying in combat that no battle plan survives first contact with the enemy. You can only be as prepared as you are aware.

- **Scalable:** Most inventors never consider the scale problem, or what will happen if their innovation takes off. Are you prepared to scale up or down as necessary?

+ **Strategic:** Every move you make should advance you toward your goal. Sometimes what looks like retreat is nothing more than regrouping. Knowing where you plan to be in three months, six months, a year and five years and building enough flexibility into the plan to develop "what-if" scenarios helps you create a strategy.

+ **Clear:** If you can't explain the gist of your plan in thirty seconds, your plan may not be a good one. This doesn't mean it's automatically or inherently bad or flawed, but it does mean that you haven't refined it down to the point where a child could follow your steps and see where you're going.

This is where the Master Mind comes in. By applying each member's unique strengths and perspectives to the plan, you can gain a greater degree of foresight, which is key to preparation. Once that happens, you can craft a plan with enough agility to pivot, but which remains robust enough to be sustainable in the face of any number of possible difficulties.

In the original *Think and Grow Rich*, Napoleon Hill emphasizes the planning and sale of services. Ultimately, everything you produce, whether tangible or not, is a service. Troy Faletra's ThrowRaft is a service with significant lifesaving capability. The java sleeve is a service that prevents burnt fingers. My firm is a service that helps inventors navigate the often murky waters of patent law. It is this service-based perspective that allows for the best presentation of the product to the general public.

One of the great flaws in my plan was the prospective lack of income I would face while launching my own firm. However, I had an ace in the hole to resolve that problem as well. All I needed was a little luck and the right person in the right place.

As it happens, I had both.

When I was in law school, I had come to the attention of Professor Jim Wilets. Jim was a brilliant scholar of Constitutional law and his passion for human rights work was contagious. He taught a course on equal protection under the Constitution, and I signed up even though it had absolutely nothing to do with patenting. Jim kept office hours and encouraged students to come by if they had any questions about the coursework or material. I often would visit and we would discuss some of his writing and other work relating to human rights. I would talk about my career goals and I had confided to Jim about the desire to move to New York and work for Fish & Neave. In most circles, verbalizing that I wanted to work for the law firm that patented the Wright Brother's airplane, Thomas Edison's lightbulb and Alexander Graham Bell's telephone would be met with incredulity.

Jim was different.

Here was a Constitutional scholar who had studied at Yale and Columbia, telling me not only that I had what it took to apply to Fish & Neave but demanding that I do it.

When the day-to-day struggles of working full-time and going to school in the evenings and studying half the night would wear me down, I would go and speak with Professor Wilets. A bundle of positive energy and all heart, he was the gasoline I needed when I was running on fumes. This period of my life reminds me of the famous poem, Footprints:

Footprints

One night I dreamed a dream.
As I was walking along the beach with my Lord.
Across the dark sky flashed scenes from my life.
For each scene, I noticed two sets of footprints in the
sand,
One belonging to me and one to my Lord.

After the last scene of my life flashed before me,
I looked back at the footprints in the sand.
I noticed that at many times along the path of my life,
especially at the very lowest and saddest times,
there was only one set of footprints.

This really troubled me, so I asked the Lord about it.
"Lord, you said once I decided to follow you,
You'd walk with me all the way.
But I noticed that during the saddest and most trou-
blesome times of my life,
there was only one set of footprints.
I don't understand why, when I needed You the most,
You would leave me."

He whispered, "My precious child, I love you and will
never leave you
Never, ever, during your trials and testings.
When you saw only one set of footprints,
It was then that I carried you."

Professor Wilets had not only encouraged me to pursue my dream of joining Fish & Neave, but he had also often enjoined me to consider teaching, a subject he was unbelievably passionate about. Years later, when Jim was a professor at Nova Southeastern Law School, he was instrumental in getting me in as an adjunct professor there. The pay was a pittance, as adjunct professors without tenure have an average shelf life measured in nanoseconds on the academic time scale. However, I quickly saw where Jim's passion for teaching came from and found being in front of a classroom incredibly addictive. I had actually flown from New York to Florida a couple of times at my own expense to serve as a guest instructor in Jim's classes and the experience was unbelievable and I was hooked for life.

Since I'd never stood on the professor side of the podium outside of class projects before, I wanted to make the right impression. The fact that I was actually younger than many of my students added a bit (okay, okay, a lot) of extra pressure. Professors in law school frequently wear suits, but on my teaching days, I made it a point to step my game up by wearing the crispest suit I had and being in class fifteen minutes early so I could stand up front by the podium so that there would be no questions as to who was running the class.

It was my first taste of teaching...and I adored it to no end.

Now I sent Jim a brief email, outlining what I was planning and inquiring about continuing as an adjunct professor after I relocated back to South Florida. The thought of not having any clients when I went out on my own was daunting. Teaching as an adjunct helped quell these fears and would also help me to make important contacts in the legal community and gain instant credibility among other lawyers. My plan still felt like madness, but at least I now had something to bring to the plus side of the ledger when I approached the next hurdle: convincing Saba.

At this time, Saba was not working, making us a "two professionals, no income" family if I proceeded with the plan. Our eldest daughter was barely two years old and my wife and I were expecting our second, with my wife seven months pregnant. How does one tell one's wife that he's planning to quit and launch his own firm with no clients, no office, no savings, no health insurance and no "plan B?"

Taking a deep breath, I sat her down and drew her through it step by step. But, I said, Jim Wilets had my back and in fact I'd already broached the subject of teaching at Nova Southeastern Law School for a while. We wouldn't be making the wads of cash we'd gotten used to, but it would at least give us some secure income while I played the long game with the practice. I sat there, waiting for her to scream at me for my idiotic daydreaming and assure me that I was jumping off a cliff…and asking my entire family to hold my hand on the long drop to the bottom. She heard me out and then gave me the last reaction I would ever have expected.

"So, tell me about your partner."

I'd mentioned Glenn to her many times, but in the context of a friend, not as a prospective business partner. I'm not sure why, looking back. Maybe I wanted to keep an ace in the hole if I needed it. Maybe I didn't really believe enough in the dream of my own firm to want to put him out that way in front of Saba. I'm sure my reasons made sense at the time, but I couldn't begin to explain them now.

"Oh, well, his name is Glenn, we went to law school together, and took the patent bar examination while still in our second year of law school. Both of us passed it on the first attempt. We split gas and drove up together to Orlando to take the exam. Remember? My friend from law school that I talk to every couple of months?"

She gave me an arch look. "Okay, but that doesn't tell me much about him."

"What do you want to know? The guy looks like Christopher Reeve. You know – Superman. He is tall, thin, doesn't drink, doesn't smoke and tells the truth."

"Sounds like a 'man crush' to me," she said, a smile breaking over her lips.

"Ha-ha! Funny," I retorted, giving her a quick peck on the cheek.

"And hey! You've got the perfect name for your practice."

"Huh?"

"John Glenn."

I didn't get it, and said as much.

"You know…the astronaut?"

"Well, we're definitely exploring uncharted territory," I conceded. She pulled me close for a longer, lingering hug.

"Do what will make you happy," she said when we parted. "I believe in you and I love you."

Fortified by Saba's matter-of-fact acceptance of my madness, I called Glenn Gold.

"Hi, Glenn. It's John."

"What's going on?"

"I'm doing it."

He paused for a beat. "Doing what?"

"I'm quitting Fish & Neave and coming down to join you." Glenn had already resigned and started out on his own several months ago and was anxiously awaiting my arrival. He knew it was just a matter of time before I could give notice and join.

He laughed. "I was wondering what was taking you so long," he finally said, "Okay. Get down here!"

I wanted to brand our new firm as "The Idea Attorneys," and ran the idea by Glenn.

"It's an okay name," he said matter-of-factly, "but what makes you think you're the first patent lawyer in the country to think of calling himself an idea attorney?"

"We can't just assume it's taken," I shot back. Then I added, "Let's do what we would advise our clients to do. Let's not give up on the idea until we have done a search and confirmed that 'The Idea Attorneys' is not available. All we need to do at this point is to check and see if there are any conflicting trademarks."

"Okay I'm fine if you want to take this on as a pet project," Glenn replied. His tone suggested we had a better chance of winning the lottery than getting the right name.

He is probably right, I thought to myself. *What are the chances that us two young twerps are the first patent attorneys in the country to have ever thought to call ourselves "The Idea Attorneys?"*

It only made sense to do a search. Hell, we are intellectual property attorneys and the search doesn't cost us a dime. It was just a matter of taking the time to do it.

And so I stayed up all night that night running every single variation of "the idea attorneys" I could conceive of through the trademark database. "Idea Attorneys," "Idea Lawyers," "New idea Lawyers," "Idea Counsel."

"The Idea Attorneys" was available. I had a winner.

"Now to apply for the trademark," I said, pulling up the relevant site. I started to enter the information, determined to get there first.

The power of the auto-suggestion was so strong that I couldn't help but take action towards my goal. I began preparing for my departure from the firm by signing up for the Florida Bar Exam. I registered the trademark for my firm, The Idea Attorneys® and got the domain name. I began working on my website every spare moment that I had.

I had a burning desire to go out on my own and I took the steps towards that goal as if on auto-pilot. I credit that to the auto-suggestion firmly implanted in my mind by that ambulance on that one fateful morning at 1251 Avenue of the Americas.

The gray twilight rolled back a little, and somehow I knew if I ran at full throttle, hard enough and long enough, I would escape it altogether. I just had to give myself no other option but to go full out or stay put, and I'd already chosen.

With so much fortune, I decided to add one more name to the Master Mind roster.

And it almost proved disastrous to my plan.

Jim Wilets, my old mentor and friend, emailed me back and said he'd be delighted to support my application for adjunct professorship at Nova Southeastern. The relative ease with which things were happening frightened me a little, to be honest. It almost felt a little too easy. Saba, Jim, Glenn and my family were all on board. The only naysayers were the ones who weren't going anywhere or doing anything different anyway.

Exhausted from the long night, I trudged into work the next day and gave my two weeks' notice. My first day on my own, symbolically enough, was July 4, 2001, Independence Day and the day after Saba's and my wedding anniversary. I was finally pursuing my own dreams, and the day I gave my notice was the last day in my life that I actually felt like I was working.

Napoleon Hill talks about the importance of having a good mate in *Think and Grow Rich*. "A man's wife may either make him or break him," Hill wrote, and he was absolutely right. I will eternally be grateful for her faith and belief in me, and her willingness to support my dream at a time when I could scarcely believe in myself. Saba wasn't the issue, nor was she the prospective member of the Master Mind who would prove problematic.

I ran the branding concept by an experienced attorney that I knew to get his thoughts on the name. Tony, an older and much more experienced sole practitioner

101

that I knew and trusted, had left a large prestigious law firm years ago and I felt that he was a good source for advice on quitting Fish & Neave to go out on my own.

"You guys are just starting out with your new firm," Tony said. "A name like 'the Idea Attorneys' is going to be a turn-off for a lot of potential clients that have needs that are not strictly related to patenting. What about all the simple legal tasks that come your way like forming a corporation, reviewing a simple lease, drafting a simple will?" He stopped for a moment and gave me an arch look. "Who is going to go to the freaking 'idea attorneys' to get a will?"

He took a deep breath and stared at the wall for a while before turning back to me. I knew him well enough to hear the gears turning in his mind, and kept silent. Soon he turned back, ticking off points on his fingers.

"You have no clients," Tony mused. "You have no savings, you are virtually unknown in South Florida and so nobody is going to refer you work."

"Tony, I didn't quit the best patent law firm in the United States so I could form a corporation or do a simple will," I replied, incredulous at the suggestion.

"Well, you didn't quit the best patent law firm in the United States to starve to death either, did you?"

I let the words sink in. Perhaps Tony was right. I propped my chin on my fist and turned the problem over in my mind.

We could start out without branding ourselves as "The Idea Attorneys." We could initially do simple contracts, wills, no-contest divorces, help people fill out legal forms, help small landlords with lease agreements and eviction proceedings and perhaps take on the occasional traffic ticket case just to make ends meet. It would mean doing all the parts of legal practice that bored me senseless in law school, but at the very least it would ensure we didn't go hungry until the serious clients starting coming. Once we were more established we could always change our firm's branding to "The Idea Attorneys."

On a practical level, Tony had a point. But practicality aside, the idea of setting myself and Glenn up as anything other than The Idea Attorneys didn't ignite my passion or my excitement. It just didn't feel right.

I thanked Tony for his time and left, thinking once again about that quote burned into my sub-conscious:

Far better it is to dare mighty things, to win glorious triumphs even though checkered by failure, than to rank with those timid spirits who neither enjoy nor suffer much because they live in the gray twilight that knows neither victory nor defeat.

If I was going to make it, I decided I was not going to drop "The Idea Attorneys." I was either going big or not at all.

And that die had already been cast.

This illustrates the importance of having a Master Mind that not only understands and is enthusiastic about your plan but whi can also help you understand the flaws in it. The problem with this, as demonstrated by Tony's words above, is that a certain amount of pessimism is a useful trait. Too much of it becomes toxic. Likewise, optimism can be equally dangerous in its own right. The wise innovator develops a keen sense for knowing which advice is worth heeding and which isn't.

Tony had experience, a solid practice and good points. But if I'd listened to him, I would not be where I am today, doing the thing I love. I'd be up to my eyeballs in estate planning and corporation formation, dabbling in patent law when I had time.

Choose who you listen to and when very carefully, because the right word at the wrong time could make all your organized planning for naught. Thomas Edison "failed" times before he created a working electric light bulb. When he was asked how it felt to fail that many times, he is reported to have said, "I didn't fail. I learned ten thousand ways not to make a lightbulb." He had the flexibility and determination to work his organized plan until it yielded legitimate results. Your plan should have qualities of both.

Chapter Takeaways

1. Build a Master Mind of people who will help you work toward success while noticing possible roadblocks.

2. Have a plan that is actionable, flexible, aware of potential problems, scalable and clear.

3. Choose who you listen to carefully, for better and worse.

4. Plan your work and then work your plan.

"It's hard to lead a cavalry charge if you think you look funny on a horse."

— Adlai E. Stevenson II

7

Leadership: What Is It?

You see it on LinkedIn every day, or at least every other day. "What does it take to be a leader?" You might think you already know what it takes to be a leader. After all, you left or are in the process of leaving something you know for something you don't and encouraging other people to come on the trip with you. What is that, if not a leader?

Napoleon Hill identified eleven traits of a successful leader.

1. They have unwavering courage based on self-confidence.

Leaders believe in their vision and are confident enough in their vision to see it through. They can also inspire others to do the same by their example.

2. They have self-control.

A true leader doesn't overreact. The leader evaluates, assimilates and assesses without giving in to strong emotional reactions.

3. They are fair.

A true leader has an innate sense of justice and fair play. This means not praising where it's not earned and not punishing when it's not appropriate. The best leaders are those who reward or discipline according to the needs of the person in question and according to a basic sense of right and wrong.

4. They don't wait for perfect answers to make a decision.

Great leaders are not and cannot afford to be risk-averse. They are willing to take chances based on the best available information, rather than trying to wait until every possible variable and variation is locked down and carved in stone. Leaders don't get bogged down in minutiae and trivia.

5. They work by a plan.

Leaders often speak of their instincts or gut feelings, but these by themselves are never the crux of a decision. The organized plan a leader builds and follows determines the degree of success the leader can expect to achieve.

6. They do more than what is required.

A true leader is never content with "good enough" and constantly strives for both self-improvement and the improvement of their followers. This person doesn't feel that any task, no matter how menial, is beneath them. Leaders validate the experience of their people by demonstrating their willingness to do more and work harder than they demand of their people.

7. They are exceptionally likable.

A leader doesn't have to be everyone's best friend, but cultivates a genuinely pleasant personality and demeanor. The best leaders read as honest, sincere and dedicated and inspire others to be the same by demonstrating the benefits that accrue from this perception.

8. They have empathy.

Good leaders understand that each person is unique and that what works for one person may not be the right or best solution for another. These people strive to understand the needs, desires, problems and personalities of the individual and integrate them on their own terms, rather than trying to force the individual to conform to an outside ideal that inevitably causes resentment.

9. They pay attention to detail.

Leaders don't get caught up in minutiae, as I said before, but they do sweat the small stuff. A good leader knows how to evaluate between small but critical details and differences that make no difference and therefore are no difference. There is "no job too small" for a true leader.

10. They assume full responsibility for their team.

When their people fail, the leader assumes responsibility for the failure. When their people succeed, a leader leaves the credit to those who crafted the success instead of taking all the glory for the leader's own. "The successful leader must be willing to assume responsibility for the mistakes and the shortcomings of his followers," Hill writes. Successful leaders own their team's mistakes instead of "passing the buck."

11. They are cooperative.

Leaders bring a mindset of harmony and unity to their business and their lives. To the true leader, there is no such thing as "us versus them" within the team environment. There is only "us." By demonstrating this effectively and in an ongoing manner, leaders foster a positive environment for growth and inspire others to do the same. More importantly, a leader establishes a team of people who can manage the things that are beyond the leader's scope in a way that breeds mutual benefit.

When a person invents something new, that person by default steps into a leadership position. The trick is not to confuse being a leader with being a tyrant. People will not willingly follow a tyrant for long simply because tyrannical rule will inevitably chafe at those under the tyrant. A tyrant rules through fear, aggression and punishment. A leader governs through cooperation, empathy and reward.

At its core, invention is leadership distilled to its simplest and most basic terms. The inventor has a perception of need and develops a solution to that need. Then the inventor inspires others to not only see the need, but understand that the inventor's solution is the correct one for that need. This is nothing more or less than leadership.

By making the conscious decision to solve a problem personally, rather than waiting for someone else to solve it for them, the innovator by definition self-eliminates from the ranks of the followers. The innovator may have been a follower prior to the act of invention, but automatically becomes a thought leader once the initial plan for success is created.

This doesn't mean that the innovator automatically becomes a de facto leader, only that the innovator has demonstrated leadership. The other qualities that define a leader must be present at least to some degree or the inventor cannot expect to get very far with their creation.

Now that we know what a leader should look like, how the leader should behave and what results a legitimate leader, which is to say a leader who leads with the consent of the people who follow, we should have a look at some reasons why leaders may fail.

1. Inability to organize details

We've already established that a leader need not and in fact should not attempt to be a polymath, or someone who wears many different hats. While a leader can and should be aware of at least the broad strokes of everything everyone in the organization is tasked with, the leader's primary concern should be organizing details so the followers' jobs are as streamlined as possible. Leaders who let details slide tend not to remain leaders, as evidenced by the number of *coups d'etat*s and mutinies among kings, dictators and corrupt governance of all kinds throughout history.

2. Unwillingness to do that which you ask of others

A leader never asks the people they command to do something they are incapable of or unwilling to do themselves. Most everyone has had this boss or that professor who proved by their words and actions that they wouldn't touch the chore they were handing out with a twenty-foot pole, but expected the people placed under them to be grateful for the opportunity. This is not leadership, but tyranny. The good leader stays in touch with the demands placed on the followers and does what can be done to alleviate them when and where necessary. Above all else, a leader should serve as an example that no job is too small or unimportant for the leader's personal involvement and is therefore not too small or unimportant for the people engaged to do the task in the leader's place.

3. Expectation of pay for what you know rather than what you do

Knowledge without action is meaningless. This is why we say that "ideas are worthless." They aren't... but without action behind them, they are so much wasted energy and nothing more. One cannot expect to be compensated for being an "idea factory" if none of those ideas ever come to anything tangible or useful. It's where the rubber meets the road and the innovator's idea becomes something concrete, valid and useful that it also becomes valuable. Likewise, a leader who cannot put ideas into effective action can neither expect to be followed nor compensated for knowledge in and of itself. By making ideas living, breathing entities through the medium of observable action, the leader proves the compensation they earn has BEEN earned rather than merely gifted or claimed by fiat.

4. Fear of competition

One of the most effective acid tests in a leader is how the person reacts to competition. A real leader says "Bring it on. I'm ready." A false leader or despot will find reasons or excuses not to engage or to eliminate the competition through means fair or foul, so long as the leader's dominance is not challenged. Leadership is not something that can be conferred once and remains from then on. It can and will be taken from the person who is afraid to continuously earn the right to be a leader. True leaders deal fairly with those on their team as well as those from other, even opposing interests. This does not mean the leader cannot or should not be ruthless in their dealings, so long as the dealings are demonstrably fair and just in their concept and execution.

5. Lack of imagination

Of all the sins a leader can commit, this may be the worst. A leader can be forgiven many other flaws, but squeamishness or unwillingness to look beyond their narrow bandwidth and explore new possibilities is not one followers readily overlook or ignore. Timidity is not and has never been a valued leadership trait, and the inability to employ imagination to see both the potential positive and negative outcomes of a situation isn't either.

6. Selfishness

A true leader is more invested in how a given situation affects everyone than the leaders own narrow agenda. This is one reason why many American voters are so disenchanted with the US Congress these days. Big Oil and the IRS are actually better-liked and approved of than the body politic that purports to govern the United States of America[5]. The reason why is simple: the American people by and large believe that the members of Congress are willing to do anything, even sell out their fellow Americans, in the service of their own ongoing electability and self-interest. Similarly, a leader who is more interested in keeping and consolidating power than looking out for their followers can expect to lose the confidence of those followers and sooner or later the right to be considered a leader.

7. Intemperance and overindulgence

Much like selfishness, these qualities bespeak a leader who is too self-absorbed to be effective. Leaders who throw a temper tantrum when things go wrong or who drink too much and "party too hardy" at the company holiday social are both likely to be viewed as buffoons who do not deserve their title. A leader should first, foremost and always be cognizant of the example

[5] Jim Newell, 2011. "The IRS Is More Than Four Time More Popular Than Congress" *Gawker*. http://gawker.com/5860272/the-irs-is-more-than-four-times-more-popular-than-congress

they set and the way their behavior reflects both on themselves and the people who follow them. No one will willingly follow an idiot, nor will they follow someone who indulges themselves at the expense of the people who serve them and in turn should be served.

8. Disloyalty

A disloyal leader is easy to identify. This is the "leader" who always has an excuse or fixes blame instead of the problem. This so-called leader will throw followers under the bus readily instead of accepting ultimate responsibility for both follower's successes and failures. A leader who betrays their followers will soon be identified, and the loss of any prestige, honor or favor they have earned is no more than a short step beyond.

9. Emphasis on the "authority" of leadership

Authority is not something than can be effectively taken, only given. Every leader who has ever forgotten this has lost the right of rule in relatively short order. The effective leader acknowledges and keeps uppermost in their mind that they only lead by the sufferance of their followers. King George forgot this, and lost the lion's share of the North American continent to his erstwhile subjects during the American Revolution. People who rule through "authority" really mean to say they rule through fear. Authority comes from one's actions reflecting one's ideals in a positive way at all times. Anything less is not authority at all, but fear, and rule through fear cannot endure.

10. Emphasis on title

Titles mean something. Otherwise they would not exist. However, it is self-evident to the true leader that relying upon the office and authority of a title rather than one's own innate ability to inspire is a fool's errand. When people in the military salute those of higher rank, they are showing respect to the office and title the higher-ranking person carries, not necessarily to the person themselves. This type of respect is obvious because it's pro forma, not extended from genuine admiration. Titles mean something…but if the person carrying the title cannot inspire admiration and willing obedience effectively, that person also cannot rely on the inherent authority of a title, lofty though it may be, to sustain that person.

The solution to poor leadership, says Hill, is to first keep in mind the eleven positive traits of a leader and strive to emulate them every day and in every situation. This is not always possible, because human beings are inherently frail and messy creatures. What is called for here is honest effort, not perfection. The secret is, when a leader errs, the leader owns the error and sets about to correct it instead of attempting to excuse it.

However, there is a second step to this. This step is what Hill calls the QQS formula. QQS stands for "Quality, Quantity, Spirit." Let's examine this more closely.

"Quality" is the way in which the leader delivers work. This extends to not only the craftsmanship and materials used to create the end product, but the ethos with which the product is created. Quality is a buzzword that gets thrown around so much it has all but lost meaning in the mind of the public, like most buzzwords do. Still, it remains the hallmark of both invention and leadership because it concretizes the pride the inventor and leader justifiably feel in their own innate capabilities and those of the people under them.

"Quantity" is the amount of work done over a given period. A leader should be willing to work harder and more diligently than anyone who follows them. This doesn't mean working around the clock or trying to have a finger in every pie. It does mean setting a standard that both the leader and the followers can be proud of and one that provides the service or goods to the public that is expected by all sides.

"Spirit" means not just how the job is done, but why. The idea of customer service, much like quality, has become yet another overused buzzword. However, when a product is created in a spirit of service to the public, the followers and the leader alike, everyone benefits. Thus we see that "spirit" is another way of saying "cooperation" taken in this context. In nature, cooperative predators are the ones who are most likely to be successful. In the human species, cooperation is what has given us the culture we live in, for better or worse. People who bring the spirit of cooperation rather than ruthless mercenaryhood to their work and dealings with others are the ones who are best adapted to survive, to borrow Darwin's phrasing.

People who neglect the QQS formula or who embrace the ten fallacies of poor leadership are likely also suffering from one of the thirty excuses for failure that Hill codified. We've all used at least one of these excuses in our lives at some point. I certainly know I have! The difference between the successful person and the failure is that the successful person stops giving themselves permission to fail and replaces that permission with the God-given right to succeed.

Yes, I said "right." It's not a privilege. It's not something that happens to someone else. When you give yourself permission to succeed and claim success as nothing more or less than your birthright, then and only then will you be able to lead yourself forward to the reward you deserve and have earned.

The thirty excuses for failure are almost universal and so just about any "reason" someone can come up with for failure probably falls somewhere under this rubric.

Leaders who rely on these excuses when things go pear-shaped, as they inevitably do at some point, are setting themselves and their entire organization up for further failure by giving themselves permission to place blame somewhere other than with themselves. The thirty excuses for failure are:

1. Unfavorable Hereditary Background.

The idea that people are somehow "lesser" because of divergences such as autism or their racial or ethnic background has been thoroughly debunked. The truth is everyone is a genius and/or incredibly skilled at something, and everyone has an area in which they fall short. This idea is reprinted here solely to make the point that while this was considered valid in Hill's time, today we know better and therefore this is nothing more or less than an excuse to fail.

2. Lack of a Well-Defined Purpose in Life.

Not everyone can or should be a prophet, a magnate or a world leader. However, everyone who has become anything ever in the history of the world has had a well-defined purpose. Those who choose failure or to complain about their bad breaks instead of doing something about them are the only truly hopeless cases that ever existed. Drug addicts, people who lose their fortunes and livelihoods to habits like gambling and people who start from poor environments can overcome this by simply finding a purpose and sticking with it, no matter what.

3. Lack of Ambition to Aim Above Mediocrity.

This should be self-explanatory. Anyone who doesn't care enough to do more than the minimum required to "get by" cannot expect to achieve the things someone who feels and strives to achieve a higher calling or purpose can. For this person above all, Hill rightly said there is no hope whatsoever.

4. Insufficient Education.

Henry Ford's example, described earlier in this book, disproves the idea of "education" as a means to success. Ford had all the education he required to achieve his goals and objectives. Education is nothing but a group of accumulated facts. How these facts are used and brought to bear to achieve a tangible result is what counts, not the level of academic progress or credentials one attains. Educational gaps can be filled through other people's knowledge when and where necessary, but the inventor need not and should not be a polymath in order to be successful.

5. Lack of Self-Discipline.

Napoleon Hill said, "If you do not conquer self, you will be conquered by self." and his point is well-taken here. Before you can command others or control the countless variables of the inventive process, you must first master yourself and your reactions to both favorable and unfavorable conditions. Thoughts become actions, actions become habits. If your habits favor self-discipline, they will inevitably lead you to success.

6. Ill Health.

Good mental and physical health are essential to the successful person. Limiting or cutting out intake of junk food, cigars and cigarettes, alcohol and other such substances while taking regular exercise and engaging in activities that stimulate both the body and mind are essential facets of achieving the kind of health that fuels success. Hill advocates for control of the sexual urge, which we will examine further in another chapter, and there is some validity to this. However, this does not mean one need or even should be celibate in order to achieve success. As with everything else, moderation is the key.

7. Unfavorable Environmental Influences During Childhood.

There is a rule that people become the average of the five people they spend the most time around. During childhood, when we learn most of our social habits, is the time that we are most likely to develop the habits we carry with us into adulthood. However, there is also a school of thought that says we change roughly half of our social circles every seven years. By this logic, by the time someone reaches the age of 28, that person's social circle should have completely changed at least twice. Therefore, there's always a chance to overcome this with the application of willpower and the right influences.

8. Procrastination.

We've all seen that person who sits at a traffic light waiting for the exact perfect shade or tint of green before they'll step on the accelerator, the coworker who's always fifteen minutes late (and always has a "really great reason!") or the schoolmate who never seems to get their classwork in on time. Procrastination is the most common cause of failure, and it's also the easiest to overcome. The application of self-discipline and willingness to start projects *now* instead of "at the optimal time" is all we need to kick the procrastination habit and start making progress. The best time to start was yesterday; the next best time is *now*. Start *now*!

9. Lack of Persistence.

Finishing what you start is the hallmark of the leader and the truly successful person. This is one of the places where most people fall down. Things get "hard." Life gets in the way. Roadblocks and challenges that seem insurmountable crop up. The difference between a successful person and a failure is how these problems are dealt with and how diligently the person works toward the desired outcome.

10. Negative Personality.

Like attracts like. Positivity attracts positivity and thus prosperity. Negativity attracts negativity. People with negative personalities cannot hope to attract positive people and therefore prosperity. This can be faked for a while, but sooner or later the truth will always come out. By emphasizing positives and trying to remember to look at the pluses of a situation rather than its drawbacks, this can be dealt with. To be sure, it's one of the hardest things on this list to manage. Some people spend a lifetime trying to change their outlook on life without success, but for those who can manage it, an entire vista of previously inconceivable possibilities reveal themselves.

11. Lack of Controlled Sexual Urge.

After eating and before dying, sex is the most basic and natural thing human beings do. Because of this, the biological imperative to perpetuate the species through sex (regardless of gender or orientation, the same basic drive is in play) is the most powerful hunger we have besides hunger itself. When the sexual urge is not properly controlled and directed, it can spill over into other parts of our lives and deprive us of a creative power so potent and fundamental that many people never realize or notice it for what it is. By controlling and redirecting the sexual urge into other forms of creativity and invention, we can harness an incredible force for the generation of innovation, wealth and success.

12. Uncontrolled Desire for "Something for Nothing."

The gambler, the person who sits around with their hand out waiting for the world to care for them and the person who plays the stock market with more money than they can afford to lose are all prone to this desire. *the world owes you nothing but a chance.* What you do with opportunity when it arrives is entirely up to you. When you make the error of expecting something of value without giving anything of value in return, you set yourself up for failure. Las Vegas wasn't built on winners; it was built on the greed of people who expected something for nothing, with devastating results for far too many of them.

13. Lack of a Well Defined Power of Decision.

A true leader can evaluate current and foreseen trends and make a decision quickly, sticking by it until and unless circumstances necessitate a change in direction. A leader can be right or wrong; indecision is the Great Sin of leadership and is usually accompanied by procrastination. This pairing is inconvenient in the short term, annoying in the middle range and disastrous to long-term planning.

14. One or More of the 6 Basic Fears.

Poverty, Criticism, Ill Health, Jealousy, Old Age, Death. These are fears that every human being must face and overcome. There is no way to effectively inoculate against them except to experience them, face them and accept them for what they are. We will analyze these more in a later chapter.

15. Poor Choice of Mate.

We've all seen or been that person with a significant other, partner or spouse who's constantly nagging and complaining about everything or nothing at all. This kind of relationship is poison to creativity, because usually the person on the receiving end of the nagging will be willing to accept mediocrity in order to achieve a semblance of peace and quiet. A mate who accepts and empowers their partner to succeed is the only kind of relationship that has any hope of lasting, especially in today's divorce-prone society. Moreover, such a mate becomes the innovator's greatest ally and champion in their endeavors.

16. Over-Caution.

Someone who's never willing to take a chance is just as problematic as someone who's always ready to roll the dice. There's a happy medium between being cautious enough to evaluate opportunities for what they're worth before moving in and jumping blindly into any and everything that presents itself regardless of its actual or projected value. The gambler will always bet no matter how stacked the odds are. The investor takes the time to do an appropriate amount of due diligence before making a leap. Be an investor!

17. Wrong Selection of Associates In Business.

The surest way for a business to fail is a mix of people who associate poorly or whose work ethos doesn't mesh well. This is true between employees and employers, business partners and allies. Anyone who does business with anyone else should choose their bedfellows carefully and screen to ensure that the right qualities for continued success are highlighted in the company culture.

18. Superstition and Prejudice.

Nothing displays irrational fear and ignorance like these two flaws. Flipping a coin, knocking on wood or being afraid of someone who is somehow Other because "all X are like Y" are forms of this type of thinking. The cure is simply to educate oneself and thereby alleviate fear. On the other hand, if flipping a coin six times before you make a decision calms or focuses you on the situation and the choice to be made, there are worse things you could be doing.

19. Wrong Selection of a Vocation.

Simply put, if you hate your work, it will *be* work and you won't get any pleasure out of it. You certainly won't be a success at it. At best you'll display competence, but you won't give your best and so can't expect to receive what you're truly worth. Finding a line of work that aligns with your life goals and definition of success should be the last time your job ever feels like a job. For the inventor, this is even more clear-cut because if the inventor is doing it right, the passion for the work will more than compensate for any number of other shortcomings.

20. Lack of Concentration of Effort.

Don't be a jack of all trades. Again we turn to Henry Ford. He focused on one thing and did it really well, and brought in others to do the things he couldn't so he could concentrate his efforts where they would benefit the maximum number of people. Staying focused on your primary objective can give you the power to push through when you really need it.

21. The Habit of Indiscriminate Spending.

Fear of poverty is one of the six great fears. It's also oddly correlated to people spending more than they can afford on things they don't really need. Careful saving and calculation without cutting oneself off from basic pleasures and the occasional creature comfort can help relax and foster a mindset that leads to success without fear of losing everything. This also places the person in a position of strength when bargaining for how much to price their innovations at, a valuable commodity indeed, especially in patent circles.

22. Lack of Enthusiasm.

Ennui, apathy and lack of enthusiasm are all contagious, just like enthusiasm, excitement and joy are. A leader who can arouse enthusiasm without letting it get out of hand is both more effective and more likely to succeed than one who cannot. Equally, an innovator who is excited about their product will be able to excite and interest others in their invention.

23. Intolerance.

The true leader is concerned with fairness and justice. Where there is racial, religious or other forms of intolerance, fairness and justice cannot be said to exist. Just like the innovator who is always looking for new ideas, the leader must always be broad-minded enough to consider different points of view and perspectives, which may or may not be relevant but can certainly lead people to see things differently than they otherwise might. Active discrimination is largely illegal under federal civil rights law, but there are also very good and practical reasons not to practice discriminatory thinking.

24. Intemperance.

Today we would call this "addiction." Anything that distracts energy from innovation or promoting the success of same, including drugs, alcohol, gambling or other forms of addictive behavior are to be avoided. Remember that a leader is not only evaluated by what they do, but by how they act.

25. Inability to Cooperate with Others.

This doesn't mean you have to be a "yes-man" or decline to assert yourself when necessary. However, no matter how brilliant or skilled you are, if you cannot get along with other people you'll quickly find yourself alone and bereft of both success and friends. Very few people with any self-respect will tolerate someone who always has to have things their own way.

26. Possession of Power that Was Not Acquired Through Self Effort.

Possessions and money are just stand-ins for power. When power is inherited instead of earned by one's own efforts, it is often squandered. This is why heirs/ heiresses, lottery winners and recipients of huge lawsuit settlements frequently end up broke and/or the topic of "Where are they now?" special features. The inventor and the entrepreneur are not as likely to fall into this trap because they typically started from the bottom and earned their success, but getting too much, too soon can be even worse than never getting any at all.

27. Intentional Dishonesty.

The West Point Cadet Honor Code reads, "I will not lie, cheat or steal, nor tolerate around me anyone who does." Just about everyone's been in a situation like the often-lampooned "Does this [article of clothing] make me look fat?" or a more serious situation where they had to do something they might otherwise never consider just to keep the lights on or food on the table until the next paycheck hit. Most people will be sympathetic to the well-meaning "white lie" or a minor act of dishonesty dictated by circumstances. However, when this sort of behavior becomes a predictable pattern, no one will trust the person and there may very well be legal ramifications up to and including loss of freedom in addition to the irrevocable damage to one's reputation that ensues from a pattern of dishonest dealings.

28. Egotism and Vanity.

Having a healthy sense of self-esteem and self-worth is one thing. Looking in the mirror on one's way out the door and saying, "You know what? *I got it goin' on today!*" is one thing. When one becomes arrogant about one's skills, value or physical attractiveness, this often acts as a beacon that tells others to steer well clear of that person. Self-value and self-importance are two wildly different things, but are all too often confused for each other by people who are at least theoretically intelligent enough to know better.

29. Guessing Instead Of Thinking.

The successful inventor works from facts. "If A, then B." They deal in known quantities rather than the intellectually lazy methodology of "guesswork" or "gut feelings." While both of these have their place, they are often confused with facts by people who can't be bothered to do their homework before making a decision, especially about major moves. Success does not typically favor guesses, and when it does, it's usually a fluke that reverses itself in very short order.

30. Lack of Capital.

We've all heard horror stories about this or that promising start-up that looked poised to become a "unicorn" and tanked because of insufficient capital coupled with efforts to grow too aggressively, resulting in a bankrupt or at best severely diminished company and penniless owners. Having enough start-up capital on hand and knowing how to manage what is available is all-important to one's success, because for the inventor, the attorney and the banker alike, money really does make the world go 'round.

—

In this chapter, we have evaluated at length thequalities and traits that do and don't make a leader, how to evaluate one's innovation and the methods by which it is brought to the public and the thirty reasons people most frequently fail to achieve success. In the original *Think and Grow Rich*, this information was geared more tightly toward what today we would call the freelance entrepreneur and lumped in with the previous chapter. With all respect to Napoleon Hill, I felt the concept of leadership deserved a more thorough and minute examination then it was paid in the original work and so decided to make this the seventh step, rather than an offshoot of the sixth.

Being an innovator is the first step toward being a leader. It will not be the last. Based on the information in this chapter, how does your leadership style stack up? Will you give yourself permission to succeed, or content yourself with failure?

Only you can decide this, and it may be the single most important choice you make in your entire life.

Chapter Takeaways

1. Leaders are not granted authority by right. The true leader earns it.

2. A leader can be right or wrong, but never indecisive.

3. There are 11 essential qualities to being a true leader.

4. There are 10 ways in which a leader can fail.

5. Most failure falls into 30 broad categories with some bleedover.

6. You have the right to lead yourself to success or condemn yourself to failure.

"If forensic analysts confiscated your calendar and e-mail records and Web browsing history for the past six months, what would they conclude are your core priorities?"

— Chip Heath

8

Decisiveness: The Hallmark of Leadership

Throughout history, the decisions of certain people at key points in time have influenced the course of nations and ultimately the world. We would not think of science or logic the way we do today if Socrates hadn't chosen to drink the poisoned cup rather than renounce his teachings. If Copernicus and Galileo had decided to hide their new information about the way the universe worked, rather than risk invoking the wrath of the Catholic church, we might still believe the sun revolves around the Earth. Had Magellan not sailed around the globe and definitively proven the Earth was round, we may never have realized that our world is not, in fact, flat. America would not be a free nation in its current form if a relative handful of men had not decided for the colonies that it was time to separate from English rule.

These are just a few examples of how a decision, made at the right time and place, has shaped our world.

I've shared previously how I committed one of the errors described in the last chapter: namely, that of indecisiveness. Part of my nature that makes me good at my chosen field of patent law is being possessed of a very anal-retentive nature. The drawback to this is, when I was considering starting my own practice with Glenn Gold, I wanted to make sure I knew absolutely everything and had all my ducks marching in lockstep before I ever made a move. This could have proven catastrophic, condemning me for all time to the "gray twilight" I've spoken of previously while I planned and schemed away my own life and happiness and possibly even those of my wife and children into the bargain.

This error of deciding slowly and changing directions fast is the exact opposite of what I should have been doing, and after reading the original *Think and Grow Rich* I should have known better, to be perfectly honest. The problem was and is that this is far easier to say than it is to do. It can be damned scary to look into the unknown and take that first step, no matter how solid your plans appear on paper.

My second child, a daughter, was a month and a half old when we left New York. As we headed out of Downtown, I thought of the old map legend ancient mariners used to convey the unknown: "Here be monsters." Several of the associates had made snide comments about my precipitous departure along the lines of, "We'll hang on to your resume. You'll be back." They had told me Florida was off the edge of the map. There weren't inventors in Florida! I had no hope, no plan and I'd be crawling back soon with my metaphorical hat in hand.

Like hell I will, I thought. As the last of the Manhattan skyline dropped below the horizon in my rearview mirror, I pushed Fish & Neave out of my mind. I still remember seeing the Twin Towers fade from sight, not knowing then that I would never see them again in person. September 11th, 2001 was just around the corner, but brimming with optimism, surrounded by my family and enjoying the warm July sunshine, such madness was inconceivable as we trekked down the Eastern Seaboard and back to Florida.

Back home.

I remembered some ancient war story about a general that deliberately burned his boats after arriving onshore in enemy territory so that he and his soldiers would have no choice but to survive. Since retreat was not an option, the only way to go was forward to victory or certain doom.

And as soon as it was decided, things began falling into place.

To help make connections in the legal community and supplement my income while I built my practice, I started teaching patent, copyright and trademark law as an adjunct professor at Nova Southeastern University Law School with Jim Wilets' support. To this day, there is nothing I look forward to more than a new semester with a fresh crop of budding legal minds interested and excited to learn about intellectual property law. Teaching as an adjunct professor turned out to work well, because it gave me access to budding legal minds and contacts that I might not have otherwise had. I absolutely love everything about teaching, especially explaining complex patenting concepts in a way that makes it easy for law students to grasp.

The majority of the law students in my intellectual property class were graduating third year law students and their attention spans were short. Many already had internships or jobs lined up, so the impetus for getting a good grade in the class was not what it used to be for them. As such, I knew that if I wanted them to stay awake and pay attention in class, I had to make the patenting concepts as simple and straight-forward and easy to understand as possible. It is from this position that I took my title, "The Patent Professor" and my *modus operandi* of taking complex patenting subjects and explaining them in plain English that I developed as an adjunct professor has carried over into my law practice as well.

Although the whole thing worked out better than I felt I had any right to expect, I still started out more than a little scared, even though I knew in my soul it was the right move. What right did I have to gamble Saba's and my kids' security on my idea?

This desire to have all the information and make sure *all the things* are in the correct configuration before proceeding is human nature. It's hardwired into us. People who looked before they leapt back in prehistoric times wound up injured, dead and even eaten! Is it any wonder that millions of years of mammalian evolution has taught the human species caution, even while we know there are some lunatics out there who do things for fun that we wouldn't do unless the direst of circumstances presented themselves?

Being a leader means being willing to make a decision based on the best available information. However, it also means being willing to own the decision, revisit and reevaluate it and adjust course as necessary if it turns out the decision was a bad one. We discussed at some length in the last chapter the idea that a leader can be right or wrong, but a leader is *not* allowed to be indecisive. Followers are more likely to admire a leader with the chutzpah to make a decision and then admit it was a bad call than one who waffles endlessly over what color tie to wear to work or other frivolous nonsense.

Sound decision-making is based on these key points:

1. Being able to quickly evaluate the available information.

2. Being able to assess any gaps in the information that may influence the decision for better or worse.

3. Being able to determine what information is critical and what is not.

4. Making a firm decision in the quickest possible manner and standing by it.

5. Course-correcting only when and if absolutely necessary.

Hill lamented "today's" educational system for not teaching students how to make firm decisions, and this trend still holds depressingly true today, 79 years after *Think and Grow Rich* was first published. It's only in college that some professors even attempt to teach students *how* to think instead of *what* to think, and by that time, all too often the damage is done. On the rare occasion that a child learns to do this without outside intervention or assistance, the child is either hailed as "gifted," treated as "troubled" by educators who don't value freedom of thought and expression in their young charges, or, and most frustratingly to children and parents alike, both.

Having seen this trend for myself while teaching at Nova Southeastern University, I often shake my head at how the modern educational system seems to be shortchanging students by drilling them endlessly on rote memorization rather than giving them exercises that enhance creativity and alternative methods of decision-making. In today's world, people who cannot make decisions rapidly and defend them rigorously are virtually assured the lowest rungs of the ladder, no matter how great their innate talents are.

And yet, the modern school system seems determined to crank out "drones" at the expense of the innovation America needs so desperately to stay competitive in the context of the global marketplace.

Decision-making isn't, nor should it be, a comfortable process. After all, the more people who rely on you to make the right choice, the more daunting your decisions become. The true leader understands that even seemingly insignificant decisions can have a "butterfly effect" well beyond the specific event.

The difference between a true leader and a waffler is that the leader doesn't allow uncertainty to lead to paralysis, procrastination or flip-flopping. A leader understands that sometimes they're going to be wrong. When that happens, they own it, admit it, reevaluate and move on. They don't waste time blaming others, indulging in loud self-flagellation or trying to get out of a hole by digging up.

By this point, you're probably pretty clear on how to make a good decision by blending imagination, gut instinct and concrete facts into a choice you can live with. It's rare that our decisions will have the immediate ramifications of the choices Socrates or the Framers of the Declaration of Independence faced. When you make the choice to become an innovator and seek out the solution to a problem, you have sealed your fate.

The real question is, do you have the courage of your convictions to see it through to its logical and proper outcome? We will discuss this more in the next chapter.

Chapter Takeaways

1. Decide fast. Stand by it. Change your mind slowly.

2. You can be right or wrong. If you want to lead, you cannot be indecisive.

3. Decisions have changed more about our world than anything else. Yours may be the next world-changing choice.

4. Decisions require courage and commitment to be valid.

> *"You must keep sending work out; you must never let a manuscript do nothing but eat its head off in a drawer. You send that work out again and again, while you're working on another one. If you have talent, you will receive some measure of success - but only if you persist."*
>
> — Isaac Asimov

9

Persistence and Invention

Thomas Alva Edison had an idea.

He labored over this idea for years, through ten thousand iterations, trying to find a way to harness Benjamin Franklin's relatively recent discovery that lightning was nothing more than electricity and use that same power source to develop a consistent, cheap source of light.

After ten thousand tries, he finally succeeded.

When he was asked how it felt to fail that many times, he quipped, "I didn't fail. I discovered ten thousand ways not to make a lightbulb."

Today, a large portion of modern technology owes its very existence to one man and his persistence. If it weren't for the fact that another man, Nikolai Tesla, failed to record the entirety of his inventions for harnessing and transmitting electricity wirelessly, he might have been the hero that Thomas Edison is to modern inventors.

What Edison illustrated with his lightbulbs was persistence.

Inventors don't get to stop when they are in the grip of the innovative fever. Their desire to achieve a result doesn't take days off. It doesn't care about hunger, thirst or other human needs and drives. It simply demands release.

And it is that demand for release that fuels the inventor's persistence.

We've all heard the axiom that "Persistence pays." This is true…but only to a point.

- ✦   Persistence without a plan is arrogance.
- ✦   Persistence without desire is futility.

+ Persistence without help is folly.
+ Persistence without direction (i.e. leadership) is irrelevance.

Have you ever met a gambler on their way to Las Vegas or Atlantic City? I don't mean the casual "once or twice a year" gambler here. I mean the hardcore, professional gambler who's not happy unless there's a real risk that s/he is going home wearing a barrel.

These people tend to have persistence and what they *claim* to be a "plan." The fact is, if you have money and a "plan" or a "system," the casinos will fly you out, comp your room and generally treat you like a sultan for the privilege of fleecing you at the tables and slot machines.

In reality, the gambler has no plan worthy of the name. This type of person relies on blind luck dressed up in the clothes of the law of averages: if I play enough money at the right place, sooner or later I'll hit big. Sometimes it pans out. Most of the time, not so much.

The innovator doesn't leave things to chance. There's a plan, a goal, an objective to attain. Come hell or high water, the inventor won't stop until the goal is met or it is proven to be completely futile to even try.

Hill relates a story of a man who staked a claim to a gold mine back in the late 1800s. The man toiled for years and bankrupted himself hauling worthless rocks out of that mine and finally sold it off for a song. The new owners came in, started digging and found gold *three feet* from where the hapless miner gave up. Granted that cutting through three feet of rock and dirt is not a small feat, the fact remains that if the miner had only kept going a little farther, he would have made his fortune.

As it was, all his hard work went to making someone *else's* fortune instead. Had he just persevered a little longer, he would have achieved the payout of a lifetime and been extraordinarily wealthy by the standards of the day.

The question is, "How far is too far?"

The honest answer in the modern day is, "Probably somewhere between Thomas Edison and the gold miner."

We all know stories about people who bet their life savings on this, that or the other thing and determined to ride it out no matter what, only to lose everything when the investment or gamble failed to pay off. Venture capitalists invest in companies based not on how innovative the products are or how likeable the owners are, but how likely they are to turn a profit on the company!

This leaves the inventor in a classic catch-22: It's hard to get funding without a working model to show. It's hard to create a working model without capital. How does the innovator break through from working prototype and patent documentation to the more mundane matters, like valuation, raising venture capital and so on?

Persistence.

It's not enough that an inventor can talk a good game. One can be as inspiring as one likes, get people excited and on board, but if the working model doesn't work or people look at it and just feel confused, none of that counts for much, does it?

Even worse is when the innovator *knows* they're on the verge of something really big but can't quite get the pieces to gel. Edison would be all too familiar with this struggle and the frustration that accompanies it. From his example and countless others throughout history, we know that the basic formula for innovation boils down to:

+ Perception of need which desires (or we might also say demands) a solution
+ Knowledge
+ Imagination
+ Planning
+ Persistence

It is an exceedingly rare breakthrough in human history that hasn't come about as a result of a combination of these qualities and faculties. The discovery of penicillin comes to mind as an example, but there are very few others.

The rise of Silicon Valley and the megalithic companies and technologies that arose from it in the aftermath of the tech sector meltdown in March 2000 serves us poorly as a roadmap for the innovator. From the outside, these companies' rise appears meteoric, the stuff of fables and legends. Zuckerberg, Jobs and Gates are all name-dropped routinely within the tech and software industries with varying degrees of awe or disdain.

What we don't see, and what doesn't become apparent until these technologies burst onto the scene, is the amount of time spent in garages and hunched over dining room tables planning and working for no compensation, with no reasonable expectation that the work would be compensated at all!

All of these innovators share one key quality with Edison, the inventor of the bow and arrow and everyone who ever set out to do, create or discover anything at all: Persistence.

It doesn't take a genius or an Olympian to develop persistence. People with fairly modest tested IQs and intellectual faculties do these things routinely. What all innovators share that creates persistence is:

+ A perception of need which creates a burning desire, generally stronger than any physical need or requirement, to achieve a resolution or result

+ The ability to sort out good advice from bad, or at best irrelevant, advice from friends, family and other sources

+ The development of a Master Mind that encourages and promotes accountability for the innovator

+ A clearly articulated and organized plan

When these factors are all present, success is almost inevitable. I say almost because there is always the so-called "X-factor" that can interfere and derail even the most detailed and best-laid plans.

In the early 1990s, with the rise of the first iteration of the Internet, people were getting rich at mind-boggling rates as the virtual Gold Rush paid very real dividends. The irony of this phrasing is very much intentional, as both the 1849 California Gold Rush and the tech boom occurred in one and the same state. Kids who weren't old enough to buy beer could suddenly afford the kind of high-end cars that their classmates would have to work and save for thirty years to be able to make even a modest down payment on! Their companies became giants overnight and were thought to be "too big to fail."

Then the tech bubble burst.

Suddenly a great many of these recently-wealthy found themselves reduced to even worse circumstances than they started from. Some had to eat generous portions of crow because of things they had said about former rivals to secure employment. Some committed suicide. Some simply vanished onto the streets, current whereabouts unknown. The vast majority of their companies and holdings fell apart to form the rubble and ashes from which Internet 2.0 and the Internet of Things Era in which we currently live arose.

What set the companies that survived the tech crash apart from the companies that failed?

It wasn't liquidity. It wasn't agility. It wasn't capital.

The prime field leveler was persistence. The leaders of Yahoo, Google, Apple and so on tightened their belts and kept on doing what they did best. The leaders of AOL, Two Cow and Boo.com tried to course-correct in the middle of a minefield, losing market share at an alarming pace. They were flailing, like a drowning person thrashing about in the ocean.

And just like that drowning person, sharks soon appeared to ravage the carcasses that remained.

This seems like a good moment to detour for a moment and point out that I'm not casting aspersions against those companies that survived and managed to thrive when the dust settled by comparing them to sharks. In fact, quite the opposite! Sharks haven't had to evolve since before the dinosaurs went extinct. They are the ultimate survivors. It was the smaller fish, the ones who put on "threat displays" with little actual substance to back them up, who panicked and ended up dead and/or devoured. If you get a chance to pick, and if you've come this far you have that chance right here and now, choose to be a shark, not chum!

In the world of innovation, persistence equals survival. Capital, market access, valuation and other metrics and KPIs come and go. If you really want to be able to pick out the winners, look for the people who persist against all odds.

I recently read a story about the founders of AirBnB. These two were so desperately cash-strapped when they started that they actually hawked breakfast cereal out of their house to raise the capital they needed to launch their brand. They managed it, and redefined how and where people stay for work and play. Uber is becoming a market Titan that has the cab-driving world up in arms as of this writing. Facebook went from a tiny, "no-name" website to the industry trendsetter, completely redefining Internet commerce and advertising. Meanwhile, AOL is still holding on, but only just. Yahoo was acquired by Verizon.

The sharks in this pool aren't hard to spot, and much the way most actual ocean-dwelling sharks can be identified by their dorsal fin and head shapes, the sharks of the tech world are evident because of these three qualities:

Presence

When was the last time you went a day without having a conversation with anyone that didn't include the words "Facebook" or "Google?" If you're an entrepreneur or innovator, and since you're reading this it's safe to assume you are, the answer is probably somewhere around "I can't remember!" but I'll lay you long odds it wasn't any time in the last three to five years! That's presence.

Staying Power

These companies have weathered their fair share of storms and progressed from strength to strength. The fact they are still here after market upheavals, antitrust lawsuits, C-suite coups and mass firings demonstrates stability and staying power.

Persistence

These companies have kept doing one thing, or a small suite of things, and doing them better than anyone else has managed. Most of them started from very humble beginnings. Zuckerberg and Bezos come readily to mind here. However, they persisted and persevered against all odds until Facebook and Amazon are the undisputed 800-pound gorillas of their respective markets.

Persistence is an amazing thing, but it needs something else to transform it from mere stubbornness into an actual, visible entity. We will discuss that something in the next chapter. For now, consider how persistence has served you thus far and how it may continue to do so in the future as you progress in the development of your personal success. It is my firm belief that someone reading this book will be the architect of the "next big thing" that rises to challenge or even supplants modern industry's existing Titans to the benefit of all.

Chapter Takeaways

1. Persistence pays, but by itself, it can only take you so far.

2. Presence, staying power and persistence is an irresistible recipe for success.

3. History and fortune reward those who persist and punish those who do not.

*"Nearly all men can stand adversity, but
if you want to test a man's character,
give him power."*

— Abraham Lincoln

10

Power and Innovation

What is power to you?

This is a nebulous question because it means something a little different to each person. To Person A, power may mean the ability to influence the outcome of an election directly. Person B may view power as the capacity to walk away from work and live the life of the independently wealthy. Person C may equate power with the ability to seduce, convert or influence others to their own will and ends.

In physics, power is the time rate at which work is done.[6] In mathematics, a "power" multiplies the number by itself the number of times correlating to the value of the power, such as the ever-popular $e=mc^2$. For our purposes as innovators and entrepreneurs, we'll use Napoleon Hill's definition: Power is the result of intelligent, directed, organized planning and knowledge.

A plan by itself is inert, just like an idea. It's nothing more than a concept until it is brought to "life" through the application of power. If we accept Hill's definition of "organized knowledge" as the yardstick by which we measure power, then there are three ways to obtain it:

The subconscious

The subconscious mind is always working and alert, as we discussed elsewhere in this book. It is important to remember that the subconscious doesn't understand negatives. Thus, "I have no money" is a meaningless statement in the lexicon of the subconscious, while "I'm broke" is *not* and forms the basis of an auto-suggestion. The subconscious mind is also great at developing information we don't even realize we have into something usable. Some people have learned to access this faculty through meditation, expressions of spirituality, mind-altering substances (a practice I

---

[6] Andrew Zimmerman Jones, nd. "Power" *About Education.* http://physics.about.com/od/glossary/g/power.htm

neither advocate nor condone; I merely observe that there are people out there who swear by this method) and so-called "lucid dreaming." Which techniques you choose to employ are entirely up to you, but neither I nor the publisher will be held liable for any legal or other problems arising from unwise experimentation with any combination of these methods. As was written over the doors of the first Academy in Athens: "*Know thyself!*"

Accumulated experience

This refers both to your own experience and that of every other person who has ever written or been written about. Libraries, Google searches and your own knowledge are at their most valuable when they are combined together to form something greater than the sum of their parts.

Trial and error

Learning from others' mistakes is the best and easiest way to take in information, but as J.R.R. Tolkien wrote, "The burned hand teaches best." Sometimes we have to experiment for ourselves to find out what is most beneficial or harmful to us and our grander designs. The advantage of this method of learning is that the lessons it teaches tend to stick and stick hard, adding itself forcefully to the store of accumulated knowledge we have at our disposal.

Another way to acquire knowledge, and thus power, is through the implementation of the Master Mind. This method is unique and separate from the ones above because it does not admit or permit one to seek out knowledge alone. In fact, it demands the exact opposite: That at least one other be brought into the innovator's sphere of influence to aid and be aided by the innovator.

When a Master Mind is formed, there is the inevitable formation of a number of "metaminds" around it. This can actually be plotted mathematically, and has been by a number of occultists in modern times, including Aleister Crowley and Donald Michael Kraig. I am not suggesting anyone rush out and pick up books on esoteric occultism! They are not essential to this course, but I will offer a relevant name and title in the bibliography for those who are interested.

The mathematical progression runs as follows:

One person develops 1P, where P means mental knowledge or power. Note that at this point there is neither metamind (a subset of the Master Mind) nor Master Mind, because when only one person is present there *cannot* be either of these things, leaving aside MMPD and other such very rare personality disorders that may simulate the effect of multiple people in a single body.

Two people (potentially) develop 3P, or each individual person's 1P plus an additional P for the Master Mind thus formed by the two.

Three people (potentially) develop 7P, or each individual's 1P, 1P for the metamind formed by each 2 people (since there are three in total, this means there are three combinations of metaminds possible) and 1P for the gestalt Master Mind of the trinity.

Four people (potentially) develop 15P, or each individual person's 1P for a total of 4P, 6P for the secondary metaminds formed by each combination of two people, 4P for each tertiary metamind that can be formed from a group of four by excluding one, and 1P for the gestalt Master Mind of the quad.

You can calculate this out as far as you like. As you can see, at each step, the P value becomes greater in a predictable fashion. While it does not climb in the smooth geometric progression (1,2,4,8,16,32,64...) that Kraig speaks of in his works, it is nevertheless present.

You can use this same formula to evaluate any group relationship or undertaking in terms of how much P is being developed. (Feel free to make any puns you wish at this time.) Likewise, using this formula, you can also calculate -P, or "anti-power." This force is the inertia caused when one or more members of the Master

Mind are out of harmony with the others. The physics-minded may want to consider this force as "drag" on the potential power available caused by interpersonal "friction." The mystically inclined may view it as a group aural dampening. The mathematically oriented may see it as simple subtraction. However, when calculating -P, we must remember that it's not just the individual working at cross purposes who is affected by anti-power, but the subgroups into which that individual fits that necessarily lose P as well.

A quick example: Take our group of 4 above, with a potential P of 15. One person is not in harmony or sync with the rest of the group. Thus we know 1P is automatically lost. However, each triad that person influences (3 in total) and each pairing that person is part of (again, 3 in total) also loses potential P because of this person. Thus our potential 15P drops to a mere 8P, which doubles the potential P any one person could develop alone, but is significantly less than the maximum efficiency at which the Master Mind should be expected to run. For each person going their own way instead of the intended direction of the Master Mind, this drop in P becomes more evident as the group fractures.

This method of evaluating power and energy flow can be applied to any form of business or personal relationship effectively and its effects are readily observable. When P drops out of any unit greater than the individual, leadership and persistence are the remedies that can bring the group back to full P productivity.

As entrepreneurs and innovators, we have already decided to assume a leadership role. The key now is to inspire and orchestrate others to channel their personal P into the gestalt aim, which should ultimately result in rewards and benefits for all concerned. However, this type of leadership must be done subtly, with the view to induce the desired result, not command it. A martinet or tyrant will be of no use in this situation.

Chapter Takeaways

1. Power is the result of intelligent, directed, organized planning and knowledge.

2. Plans must be infused with power in order to transform them into tangible, functional things.

3. It is possible to evaluate the potential power of any Master Mind mathematically, and furthermore to determine and pinpoint when the Master Mind is not functioning at its peak capacity.

4. True leadership and persistence are the remedies for loss of power in the Master Mind.

"Sex is always about emotions. Good sex is about free emotions; bad sex is about blocked emotions."

— Deepak Chopra

11

Sexual Energy and Invention

We have already determined that sex is much more than simply an act people do. It is an innate part of the human animal, comprised of a biological drive to (pro)create combined with an emotional need for warmth, comfort and physical contact with another. Leaving aside the relatively small number of people who identify as asexual or agendered for whatever reason, nearly every human being is a sexual being first and foremost.

Organized religions, philosophical constructs and political institutions of all types have tried to harness, direct, control or outright purge the sexual drive from human beings, with varying degrees of success. Plato advocated for a form of eugenics in *The Republic*, in which mates would be selected for each other by those wiser than themselves and the children of such unions bred to be of service to the State in some capacity. The Catholic Church decreed sexual intercourse to be sinful, as it turned people away from God, and thus attempted to redirect that sexual energy into prayer and service to the Church. The Nazi Party took a leaf out of Plato's book and said it was the duty of every person meeting the Aryan ideal to breed so that the *ubermenschen* (literally "overmen" or "supermen") would, in a generation or three, inherit the earth.

Attempts to stamp out sexual desire altogether by various institutions have largely been unsuccessful, mainly because outside of hunger, thirst and the voiding of bodily waste, the sexual impulse is humanity's single greatest instinctual need. Unfortunately, it is also the only need we have that cannot be completely sated on one's own. To be truly satisfying and fulfilling as nature intended, a partner is needed.

Oscar Wilde famously quipped that "Everything is about sex, except sex. Sex is about power." Taking his words at face value, this is absolutely true. In any sexual encounter involving two (or more) people, there is (at least) one person who acts as the aggressor, initiator and active partner and (at least) one who plays a more passive role.

However, on another level, we discussed power in the last chapter, and I've been hinting that we would get to sexual energy and power later. "Later" has obviously now arrived.

Let me say before I go any further that I am not at all sex-averse! A lot of people seem to think attorneys reproduce by fission, like amoebae. I can assure you from personal experience and after fathering multiple children with my wife that neither of the previous statements are the case. During every pregnancy, I was deliriously happy and utterly terrified at the same time (and won't even try to speak to what was going on in Saba's mind and heart while she did the heavy lifting, so to speak). Any man who's ever been an incipient father-in-becoming knows exactly what kind of mental and emotional contortions I went through when each of my children was born.

Getting back to our dear friend Oscar Wilde: Sex is the most potent creative force known to man. Through that simple act, we have the potential to create new life. The atomic bomb is a destructive force unparalleled in human history, but it pales in comparison to the capacity human beings have to bring a new, living being into the world. When science can supplant humans and create new human beings entirely from scratch with no need for the participation of a father and mother in any form, then and only then will science truly have ultimate power.

For now, we acknowledge sex as the incredible force it is. Everything we do, the accrual of wealth, the building of monuments, the purchasing of this or that article of clothing, jewelry or conveyance, every piece of art that has ever been created, all happens and has been done because of one thing: sex.

The idea of sex addiction is not new. Napoleon Hill didn't speak of it in exactly that terminology, because the phrase had not yet been coined when he died, but the concept of misuse or overuse of sexual energy is nearly as old as the human race. When Benjamin Franklin posited his *Thirteen Virtues*, #12 read *"Chastity: Rarely use venery but for health or offspring; never to dullness, weakness, or the injury of your own or another's peace or reputation."* It's worth noting that by all accounts, Franklin was bad about taking his own advice on this score, given that he had a reputation as something of a rake in his day and especially in his later years.

An addiction is defined in the strictest possible terms as any activity that a person must do so compulsively that it interferes with one's ability to function in normal society, employment or relationships. However, the concept of sexual addiction is one that has been largely rejected by the psychological community, given that it does not occur anywhere in the DSM-V, the handbook for diagnosing psychological and psychiatric disorders. Many other forms of addiction are included, but sex is left conspicuously out of the equation in and of itself. (When paraphilias or "fetishes" are concerned, that is treated as a completely different matter from the issue of sex alone.)

Sex is known to have a great many benefits. We've already discussed its creative role in human life. Without sex (or at the very least gender), none of us would be here. However, let's look at the broad view of what sex offers to humanity:

1. The ability to perpetuate the species. (We can debate *ad infinitum* about whether this is necessarily desirable in today's world.)

2. As a therapeutic and stress-relieving agent. Sex releases all manner of endorphins, oxytocin and other natural mood elevators and calming agents within the body. This causes reduced stress and tension, promotes a sense of well-being and makes people feel more connected.

3. As a power source for innovation. Sexual drives, when transformed and channeled from their natural intended purpose into other creative acts such as invention, writing, painting, sculpting and so on, can be harnessed and redirected into sharpening and focusing one's mental and creative

processes to complete the task at hand or view the world in a new way.

Now, understand I'm not advocating that everyone everywhere should stop having sex altogether, or drop what they're doing and start having sex right here and now! As with everything else, moderation is key when it comes to sex. Having too much leads to lethargy and a literal drug high created entirely within one's own body. This is hardly a productive state of affairs. However, too little sex and the deprivation of human touch generally leads to depression, inability to focus and a lack of desire to create anything at all. As in all other things, there must be a healthy balance for both (or all) partners involved.

But when this balance is achieved and the sexual drive is channeled properly, amazing things happen. Tesla was reported to have died a virgin, not for lack of eligible and desirous ladies' attention, but because he had so completely subsumed his sexual urges into invention that he simply didn't see any need to bother with the whole business.[7] Edison, Ford and many others are alleged to have done something similar, if not on Tesla's (perhaps apocryphal) scale.

---

[7] Toria Sheffield, 2015. "Nikola Tesla Was a Virgin with OCD who Fell in Love with a Pigeon" *History Buff*. http://historybuff.com/4-strange-facts-about-nikola-tesla-to-share-at-your-next-nerd-gathering-6Q0pA9jgDgao

Napoleon Hill considered male sexuality exclusively in the original work, pointing out two facts that have been determined from an exhaustive survey of classical literature:

1. Nearly all (male) high achievers have also had highly sexual natures.

2. Nearly everything that high achievers do is done for the attention and approval of a desired, prospective or actual mate.

Leaving Hill's genteelly *laissez-faire* treatment of the feminine side of sexuality and avoidance of orientations that had either not been thought of or were dismissed as perversions in his day to one side, he makes an interesting point.

Another point that he raises is that although high achievers also tend to be highly sexual, this is not expressed by jumping into bed with every person the high achiever desires. Instead, the sexual energy that could be expended in the usual manner is turned inward and channeled to alternate acts of creation, innovation and discovery. Evidence of this can be found in the examples of Frida Kahlo, Edgar Allen Poe, Nikola Tesla, Benjamin Franklin and far too many others to recount here.

This should not be news to anyone in this day and age when you think it over for a moment. Occultists and mystics have known about the incredible power of sexual energy for millennia, employing it in prayer, healing and for any number of other pursuits. The Sufi mystics, the harlot-priestesses of ancient Rome and the followers of goddesses from a number of pantheons viewed sex as a legitimate form of prayer and the joining of people together in sexual congress to be a fitting propitiation for certain aspects of their deities. It is only now that we are starting to truly grasp just how fundamental and powerful the sexual drive really can be.

It is capable of producing miracles if it is properly directed!

Hill also codified the Ten Mind Stimuli, which I reprint here in their entirety for the sake of clarity:

1. The desire for sex expression

2. Love

3. A burning desire for fame, power, or financial gain, *money*

4. Music

5. Friendship between either those of the same sex, or those of the opposite sex

6. A Master Mind alliance based upon the harmony of two or more people who ally themselves for spiritual or temporal advancement

7. Mutual suffering, such as that experienced by people who are persecuted

8. Auto-suggestion

9. Fear

10. Narcotics and alcohol

Notice that in the vast majority of these cases, we can argue that sex or sexual tension is lurking somewhere in the background, although perhaps "lurking" is a poor choice of words. It makes as much sense to apologize for being a sexual being as it does to apologize for eating a cheeseburger or drinking water. Like anything else, sex can be misused, abused or turned aside from its intended purposes. However, used properly, sex is another form of nourishment for the body, heart, mind and soul.

So how do we use sex properly in this context?

We've already noted that sex is a restorative and relaxing agent for the body and soul. When the body and mind are properly relaxed and calm, many people including Hill have noted that humans tend to be more receptive to information. Whether this is a function of the Divine speaking into the silence, "tuning in" to someone else's mental wavelength to find the solution to a problem or simply the inner voices shutting up long enough to let the subconscious be heard is a matter of much debate, better left to the mystic and philosopher than the innovator.

What really counts here is *that* it works, not *how* it works.

Choosing the right mate is imperative to successfully channeling sexual energy. While being able to do this on and for oneself is the ultimate proof of mastery over one's total being, it is the emotion of love that truly inspires. Sex used properly is a physical expression of love, desire and pleasure in another person's company. Used improperly, it can be just as destructive to both parties as any other form of addiction or abuse and in some cases even more so.

The point is that it requires love to truly command and harness sexual energy as it was intended and designed to be used. Hill asserts that no one who has ever achieved real greatness in any field of endeavor lacked in sexual appetite. Whether this is fair or accurate in the grander scheme of humanity at this date isn't known, nor is it really relevant in context. The fact remains that where love and sex meet, there too is the potential to develop and attune the creative, inventive and receptive faculties that are too often drowned out by the mental and physical noise of our environment and our own thoughts.

The sexual power each person possesses is a unique and savage force all its own. Learning how to harness this energy increases one's personal magnetism, presence and leadership potential. In addition, it unlocks creative faculties that most people never realize they have. It is this power that can turn someone and something mundane into an extraordinary force to be reckoned with…if it is used with intent, deliberation, care and consideration for the rights and needs of others.

Chapter Takeaways

1. Sex is a powerful creative force that can be redirected into other forms.

2. Everyone has some form of sexual energy.

3. Greatness and harmony with one's sexual being seem to be inextricably interlocked based on the historical record.

4. There are a number of ways to raise, direct and utilize sexual energy.

5. Like anything else, too much or too little sex can have the opposite effect of what one intended.

"Your subconscious is a powerful and mysterious force which can either hold you back or help you move forward. Without its cooperation, your best goals will go unrealized; with its help, you are unbeatable."

— Jenny Davidow, *Embracing Your Subconscious: Bringing All Parts of You into Creative Partnership*

12

The Subconcious Is Speaking, Are You Listening?

When we talk about the subconscious in the context of invention, I'm not necessarily referring to anything mystical or difficult to understand. In this case, it's helpful to think of the subconscious as the background program, or operating system if you like, that allows your mind to run the programs it needs for daily survival and comfort. Placing the subconscious in this paradigm tends to make it a little easier to digest for the scientifically oriented mind, which is where most innovators of all stripes reside to one degree or another.

The subconscious mind remembers *everything* we see, say, feel and experience. It has been online since the moment you were born, and some argue even before that. I prefer to liken the experience of learning to downloading new software into the system. Math, science, language skills and social skills are all just applications we train our brains to receive and recognize. While this makes navigating a world with other people and beings easier, it also makes our inner lives more difficult.

Oftentimes what happens is the brain tries to run too many programs at once, especially in today's society where multitasking, although routinely debunked as a bad idea and an inefficient way to work, is nevertheless considered a valuable skill. When this happens, the mind overloads because of too many demands from too many directions.

Think about your day today. Chances are you started off the day with a list of things to do, manage, function and worry about: bills, food, clothing choices, your significant other or lack of same, your commute to work, the tasks awaiting you, meetings, schedules... and that's just in the first half hour to an hour out of bed! Makes you want to go back to sleep, doesn't it?

Do you remember what you dreamed last night or the night before?

If you do, you have been in direct communication with your mind's operating system. Instead of using Windows, for example, you actually interfaced with your subconscious through MS/DOS.

The problem with this is, the subconscious often uses symbols and indirect means to communicate. This is why there is so much debate and interest in the meaning of dreams and random thoughts: by unlocking the "code" of dreams, it is believed in many quarters that it is possible to understand what the subconscious knows but cannot communicate clearly. Dreams may be nothing more than the mind running its personal recycling program each night, clearing out the detritus of one day to prepare the mind for the new day to come. Sometimes they may have a deeper or more important function.

In this case, the trick is to figure out which is which. Some people swear that the more lucid and real the dream feels, the more likely it is to be important. Others say exactly the opposite. It's not really important which one is right for a given person. Some people don't dream at all, or at least don't remember them!

This is a somewhat roundabout way of saying that even when your conscious mind turns off, the subconscious is still laboring away in the background. Only when we shut down the "apps" that clutter and bog down our "operating system" can we really understand what it's trying to tell us.

There are a number of ways to achieve this:

+ Finding a quiet place

+ During or immediately after sex

+ Sleeping

But did you know you can actually access the subconscious while you're awake and lucid?

Yogis and other mystical sorts have been doing this for the entire existence of humanity. In most cases, they argue that the subconscious is much more and less than an operating system. They would have it that the subconscious is the link between the Divine and one's own mind. I find it useful to think of this link as an Ethernet cable that leads to something beyond myself. What it is, I cannot say with any authority, but I know it's there.

This "something" has been given many names over the course of human history. Some examples include:

+ Nirvana.

+ Enlightenment, in the Buddhist sense.

+ The Akashic Record: the stored memories of all of humanity; think of an immense database containing the second-to-second lives of all 108 billion human beings estimated to have ever lived to visualize this.

+ The Collective Unconscious: Jung's version of the Akashic Record, limited to the experiences and knowledge of every *currently living* person.

+ Ain Soph: Pronounced "Eye-in Soaf," this is a Hebrew word which literally means "no thing." Its appropriateness in this list is subject to debate, because if there is "something," there cannot by definition be "nothing," but this is a potential philosophical wormhole well beyond the scope of this book.

+ The Knowledge and Conversation of Our Guardian Angels: this idea, brought into modern form by the Order of the Golden Dawn[8], proposes that each of us has a guardian angel and through the subconscious can actually speak to this being to determine what Divine Will has decreed for us.

+ Infinite Intelligence: this is Hill's own term for the "something" beyond the subconscious and seems to incorporate elements of all of the foregoing in some form.

[8] See Kraig's *Modern Magick* for more on this.

For our purposes here, let us assume that this "something" beyond ourselves is as real and tangible as the device on which you're reading this book. If so, it is logical to assume that this "something" must have some way to interact with us, and we with it.

So, in the interests of simplicity, let's frame our subconscious as a combination operating system and link to a database of information that we cannot properly appreciate or understand, but which is nevertheless there. If you have a paradigmatic model that suits your personal philosophy and belief structure, by all means feel free to employ that instead.

When we can shut down the apps that clutter our mental mainframe, we have access to information that otherwise cannot get through. How the information is expressed varies from person to person, because no two people experience any form of stimulus in exactly the same way. However, a number of things can either enhance or interfere with one's ability to properly access or process the information we receive through this channel. We will examine these groupings individually.

Positive emotions enhance our ability to access the information available to and from the subconscious mind. We discussed in the last chapter how sexual release can clear the mind and "free up the channel," so to speak. Sex is neutral in and of itself, but when utilized properly and with a loving spirit, it is the most potent positive force in the world. However, there are other emotional states that facilitate the ability to access the subconscious. These emotions are:

- **Desire:** "I will this thing to be."
- **Faith:** "I believe that I am the right person, at the right place, at the right time, to do this and that I have the necessary tools and capabilities to bring it to be."
- **Love:** "I act in a spirit of perfect love and trust for those I care for and all of humanity."
- **Sex:** "I turn my every desire to fuel my desire and faith that this thing will be."
- **Enthusiasm:** "I am excited and eager for this thing to be."
- **Romance:** "I will use this thing to better the lives of those I love."
- **Hope:** "I can and will do this and will prove myself worthy to do so."

Knowing this and how to clear the channel, we now turn our attention to things which can cause interference. Chances are you've already figured out what some of these are. It only stands to reason that negative emotions would be the problem, as well as extremely strong positive emotions, which can override everything else in their path.

However, I have said elsewhere that the subconscious cannot and does not process negative statements. This is true. The subconscious only understands and processes positive statements, as we see above. "I can. I will. I am." However, the subconscious is not concerned with logic, nor is the human mind a particularly consistent or logical place in its entirety. Therefore, emotions, positive or negative, are easily understood and integrated into the subconscious. With positive emotions, this is not generally a problem of any lasting duration. However, when negative emotions enter the mix, whether the statement underlying it is positive or negative is irrelevant in the realm of the subconscious.

- **Fear:** "I'm scared." "This won't work."

- **Jealousy:** "I want what s/he has." "My [whatever] isn't as nice as theirs."

- **Hatred:** "I can't stand that guy." "I really hate this."

- **Revenge:** "I'm going to get them back." "They're not going to get away with this."

- **Greed:** "I want more!" "I don't have enough."

- **Superstition:** "If I perform this (object of superstition), that will happen." "If I don't do (object of superstition), it won't work."

- **Anger:** "I want someone to pay." "I can't let this stand."

Now that we see how emotion functions in the subconscious, we know what frames of mind are best suited to connecting with and retrieving data from the subconscious. Positive and negative cannot inhabit the same space, and where negative is present, it will always prove more toxic and reactive than the positive. Developing the habit of positive thinking makes the process of engaging and maintaining a conducive frame of mind vastly simpler.

The real question now becomes, not how to access the information... but how to use it. Once we know this, we then learn how to unlock a creative potential hitherto completely unknown in our lives.

Chapter Takeaways

1. The subconscious acts as the operating system for the human mind and the conduit to the information stored beyond the mind itself.

2. The subconscious only processes positive phrases.

3. The subconscious does not process negative phrases, but it does process negative *and* positive emotions.

4. Developing the habit of positive thought can help keep lines of communication to the subconscious and the intuitive centers it controls open.

*"When the brain's potential is fully unleashed,
there can be few if any limitations. Anyone who tells
you otherwise isn't up-to-date with the latest
scientific findings on the brain and is exhibiting
their ignorance. For the brain's potential
is the human potential..."*

— James Morcan, *Genius Intelligence: Secret
Techniques and Technologies to Increase IQ*

13

Mysteries of the Brain

We all know what the brain is: a more or less orderly lump of neural tissue that transmits electrical impulses and regulates the body's biological functions. Estimates of the number of potential neural pathways in the human brain rival or eclipse the number of stars in the galaxy. Despite this, and the incredible amount of information the human brain can store, it is estimated that humans only use about 10%-14% of the brain's total capacity, and only the truly exceptional, the Einsteins, Teslas and Fermis, manage to reach the threshold of the higher number.

So what does the other 86%-90% do? Surely it doesn't just sit there!

And indeed it doesn't.

Ongoing experimentation into the workings of the human brain have revealed a lot since Napoleon Hill's time, but there's still a lot we don't understand about it. For example, we know that depression alters brain chemistry and causes areas that are usually active to become dormant. What we don't know is the mechanism that triggers it. We know that the brain can reroute around damaged areas, especially in children who suffer traumatic injury, but how and why it does this and how it "knows" which areas to work around remains a mystery.

One prevalent theory is that the brain is set up to store, receive and *send* information. This would explain a number of phenomena that we currently don't have the right scientific models to describe any other way, such as clairvoyance and telepathy.

This sounds insane when put in that context, but bear with me here.

Have you ever finished someone else's sentence, like you somehow *knew* exactly what they were going to say? Bonus points if you both said it "in stereo" and it wasn't someone you knew well.

Have you ever had a thought, described it and had someone say, "I was just thinking the exact same thing!"

Have you ever found yourself in a situation where you knew precisely what was going to happen several seconds in the future, even though the location and people around you were completely foreign to you?

Have you ever sent an email answering a question that someone else hadn't asked yet…but was meaning to?

If you answered "yes" to any of these questions, you have gotten a glimpse into one of the strangest and least understood but most incredible facets of the human mind. Telepathy, clairvoyance and déjà vu are all facets of the same ability, one that almost every human being seems to possess in greater or lesser degrees. Most people only have these things happen a few times in a lifetime, but those moments are evidence of the far greater potential of the human brain that we have yet to even begin to tap.

Before you dismiss these phenomena as mere ravings, consider that Alexander Graham Bell himself conducted experiments which seemed to strongly indicate that the human brain can function like a radio transmitter and receiver simultaneously. The American, Nazi German and Soviet governments all expended astronomical amounts of money and manpower attempting to unlock the incredible potential of the human mind in the form of psychic experimentation. Because the outcomes of many of these efforts are still classified or unknown, having been destroyed in attacks and deliberate efforts to eradicate evidence, there is no way to be certain of what progress was made. However, it would stand to reason that if something hadn't been found, the information would not have needed to be buried or destroyed.

Consider as well that a scientific bent of mind does not necessarily preclude belief or active exploration of mental and psychic phenomena. Some of the greatest minds in history were at least open to the possibility that the human brain possesses capabilities beyond our ability to accurately assess, measure or understand. If you have ever experienced any of these phenomena for yourself, whether you want to believe in them or not, rejecting them out of hand is the opposite of innovation. Remember that closed-mindedness is one of the innovator's greatest enemies.

By accessing the information and power of the subconscious, it seems likely if not inevitable that the inventor can also develop the ability to tap into areas or capabilities of the human brain that most people cannot. There are a number of ways to do this, as we have discussed in previous chapters, as well as many ways steeped in ritual and age which are beyond the scope of this book to evaluate. If you are interested in possible methods, a good starting point is listed in the bibliography for your perusal.

I would understand your skepticism at this point. But before you dismiss this part and indeed the entire book as kookery, consider what you have learned up to this point. If that much of it made sense and/or has proven effective, I ask that you give me and Hill the benefit of the doubt for just a little while longer.

We do not and cannot fully understand the brain. Unlike a computer, the human brain is, if you'll allow me a small pun, unthinkably complex. To simulate a single second of brain activity in a computer lab required 40 minutes running 82,994 processors full-out and a petabyte of system memory on what at the time was the world's fourth fastest supercomputer with a speed of over ten petaflops. All this *To reproduce one single second*[9].

Thus, we can say with a high degree of confidence that as a computation and storage facility, science is a long, long way from catching up to the amazing biological computer riding in your skull.

[9] Tia Ghose, 2014. "Supercomputer Takes 40 Minutes to Model 1 Second of Brain Activity" *LiveScience*. http://www.livescience.com/42561-supercomputer-models-brain-activity.html

JOHN RIZVI, ESQ.

Since we have only the vaguest idea of what the brain is truly capable of, it only makes sense to try to push its boundaries. As innovators, this is our highest calling and goal. If you have been doing the exercises in this book and taking them to both mind and heart, you've already been working toward this objective, whether you realized it or not.

Especially when working with the Master Mind, the goal is to reach a state of harmony and equilibrium where everyone is working toward a single purpose and focusing their entire efforts toward that end. I am not saying this book or these methods will make you psychic. I am saying that based upon Hill's techniques, you can reach a state where the line between simple sympathy or "vibing" on the same mental frequency and true psychic ability becomes very blurred and indistinct.

This sounds bizarre and even a little frightening, but it actually can be quite exciting when it happens as a result of focused, directed effort. Hill relates an experiment that determined that professional gamblers and other people whose livelihood revolves heavily around numbers seem to be able to see about three seconds into the future. The participants could not explain how they did it or the mechanism by which this ability functioned, but the results of the experiment defied statistical likelihood by such a high degree that it left the researchers in charge of the experiment convinced the outcome was valid.

When this sort of phenomenon occurs as intended, the excitement in a room becomes palpable. There may be a lot of shouting, but it's the kind of boisterous, happy shouting that accompanies a favored football team's win. People are interrupting but no one's angry, and there's a certain energy that just feels right somehow.

Of course, when it happens by accident, it can be scary or even off-putting. Everyone may look at each other, uncertain what just happened, although clearly *something* did. There is an uncomfortable sense of somehow feeling naked, bare, as if everyone has revealed something they didn't intend to and aren't quite sure how to put the genie back in the bottle or what to say or do next.

Because the human brain remains largely unexplored, it also remains unpredictable and volatile. Situations like this can be a great opportunity for bonding and cementing the Master Mind, so long as it happens as a direct result of controlled, directed and applied will. This is why understanding just how powerful these techniques can be and being prepared to apply them at the correct time and in the correct conditions, with the right frame of mind, is so vitally important to their success.

If you're thinking this sounds a lot like descriptions of the "sixth sense," you're precisely right. What you have been doing this entire time is developing a sixth sense that allows you to project and receive information to and from other people with whom you are attuned. The interesting thing about this sense is that if you practice with it, you don't have to limit its use to people you're intimately acquainted with. You will be able to pick up information from almost anyone, anywhere.

One of the most important traits of leadership is the ability to read people and sort out those who are seeking the kind of connection that will benefit both parties to the utmost. By projecting openness and honest intentions, we attract people in turn who share those qualities. The problem is that some people are predators who just want to come along for the ride but not contribute anything to the gestalt benefit of the Master Mind.

This is where these talents and skills really come in handy. They won't necessarily make you a mind reader, but they will attract those who are in sympathy with your goals and objectives while allowing you weed out those who want something for nothing. Think of this as "tuning your radar" to detect positive influences and weed out the negative. When your radar works properly, this is the "sixth sense" most people mean: the ability to recognize, evaluate and seize opportunities as they are presented, whether those come in the form of a person, situation or place. Being in the right place at the right time with the right people around you is the basic building block of success, and developing a sixth sense for attracting and sensing when the "right" elements are in place can help expedite the process of building toward the kind of success you seek.

However, the fact you've reached this point doesn't mean you get to neglect the other steps! Success and invention is a continual process of starting from square one. However, the "square one" Mark Zuckerberg or Alex Gomez starts from at this point will probably look very different from yours. Once you complete something, this end step becomes an opportunity to start again. Thus, the end of one thing becomes the beginning of another with the potential to be as big or bigger than the other!

History, fortune and success do not reward those who rest on their laurels. Einstein's theory of general relativity and the equation "$e=mc^2$" would each have been enough to cement his reputation and required him to do nothing further of any substance. Instead, he became a major contributor to the Manhattan Project, to his later regret; a physics instructor, which by his own account he loved; and published papers on a fairly regular basis.

How different might our world be today if Einstein had left off actual work and simply coasted on the strength of general relativity or e=mc²? We could argue that if Einstein hadn't noticed and codified these rules or further explored the intellectual rabbit holes they led to, someone else would have. While this is possibly true, I think it's fair to say that our world would look dramatically different, for better or worse.

Not everything requires the intellectual or mathematical talent of an Einstein. Sometimes a Gomez, Faletra, Zuckerberg or Rizvi is the right person in the right place at the right time. However, to properly evaluate this requires the known and unknown faculties of the human brain working in concert. This is the ultimate secret of success. Anything less is a cheap imitation.

Anytime you have a "hunch" or "intuition," your brain is receiving information from a source that cannot be readily identified or quantified: the subconscious. This is one of the few times that most people ever experience the subconscious directly and effortlessly. The real secret is to develop the ability to communicate with the subconscious when, where and how desired, regardless of what else is happening.

I've played a few hunches in my time, things that at the time made no sense at all but paid off beyond my expectations later. As I grow older, I also find myself becoming more intuitive. This is in keeping with what Hill said, that people don't even start hitting their stride until age 40 or later, when the sexual impulse settles enough to allow diversion into other avenues and thus fuel the subconscious.

In every aspect of human life, desire, effort, application of knowledge and brain power and the universal hunger for the closeness of sex are the prime movers that allow people to shape their own destinies, depending upon how they are used.

In *Think and Grow Rich*, Hill placed the brain and the sixth sense in different chapters. I disagree with this because it is fundamentally impossible to separate one from the other. Wire and electricity are simply assumed to go together. Without a brain and a subconscious, the sixth sense could not function, and without the sixth sense, why would we need such an elaborate storage and operational facility? Therefore, I am trying to add some clarity as to how and why I place these two things together. Consider the brain as the wire that conducts the electricity of thought, operated and orchestrated by the CPU of the subconscious, which takes its instructions from a programmer that cannot be seen or identified directly, and this scheme makes more sense because they must all inevitably work together for the system to function properly.

In the same way, the brain, subconscious, Ultimate Intelligence and sixth sense must work together, guided by human will, desire and need. Any other way is haphazard and can only lead to a useless and incomprehensible mishmash of conflicting information and desires which results in paralysis and an absolute inability to suss out the crucial points required to make a decision.

We spoke earlier of imagination. Imagination is how the faculties above examine what is and illustrate what may be to allow us to draw conclusions. Even animals have imagination of a sort, such as when a dog sleeps and begins twitching and whining in his sleep. If a dog didn't have imagination or a subconscious of its own, it would be utterly impossible for the dog to dream.

It is up to each of us to decide how those faculties will be used, or misused. Like everything else, if this innate capability is not used properly and with full awareness, it can be dangerous to the practitioner in the sense that it may work in unexpected or unintended ways, and to those around the practitioner in the sense that things may end up being revealed that would have been better left alone or may be subject to misinterpretation. Because of this, imagination and all the other faculties of the human mind must be subject to one more principle: that of *enthusiastic consent*!

By this point, you may have realized on your own that what you are attempting to do as an innovator and leader is to garner the enthusiastic consent of the people with whom you interact on any level. They must consent to back your invention. They must consent to join your social and working circles. They must consent to your leadership.

The problem is, consent is not as simple as someone saying "Yes." We all know what grudging consent looks like. It's the raised eyebrows, tight lips and tense, "Oooookaaaaaay..." that says, "I'm not really on board with your program, but I'm going to go along with it anyway." An even simpler analogy is the couple that is debating about one of them going for a night out with the boys or girls. The party not invited or welcome is unlikely to be happy about this, but wants the partner to be happy, so gives an irritated "Fine! Go ahead and go." The partner doesn't mean a single syllable of it and it's sure to lead to problems later. However, if things have come to this pass, there's probably already more trouble in the relationship than a simple evening out would account for.

As I write this, the topic of consent has reached a critical mass in American discourse because of the publicization of an alarming number of sexual assaults involving both men and women as aggressors and victims on college campuses, places which are alleged to be "safe." The idea that "yes means yes" is gaining popularity and traction over the "no means no" ethos popular even ten years ago. The caveat, of course, is that a grudging "yes" is to be taken as a "no." Only enthusiastic consent is considered an acceptable criterion for proceeding with whatever activity is being called into question.

This notion of enthusiastic consent extends well beyond the bedroom and into every facet of our lives. Consider the following points:

An employee who reports to work grudgingly but makes it clear they would rather be anywhere else, doing anything else, is not truly consenting to the work they are being paid for and will give it only the most grudging and halfhearted effort. If this sort of behavior is rewarded by the employee's salary and ongoing employment, tacit consent is being given for the employee to reap the rewards of being an employee without expending the effort that is supposedly required of the employee. Morale suffers and sooner or later, the employee does something so egregious it cannot be overlooked or simply forgets to show up for enough days that the company's "no call, no show" policy comes into effect.

A business partner who only grudgingly accepts someone's phone calls is by definition not really agreeing to be a partner. Partnership implies a state of active equilibrium, by which I mean that all partners operate in a pattern of give and take that produces an overall balance or harmony. A partner who does not contribute to active equilibrium is engaging in either active or passive destabilization, depending on how the partner's negative attitude expresses itself.

A friend who always calls only to ask for help or talk about themselves, their problems and their lives and cedes the floor to the other person with ill grace cannot be considered a friend at all. This type of person is a user and will continue to use their victims until they are used up or the "friend" grows tired of the game. A true friend listens more than s/he speaks unless invited to, and is always aware of signs of boredom or irritation in the audience.

A spouse or significant other who is always giving grudging consent for anything, from going to a movie to trying something new in the bedroom, is not truly consenting at all. Depending on what the activity is and the partner's overall attitude, this could have consequences ranging from a mild disagreement to prison time and being labeled a sex offender!

The cure for all of these potential relationship problems consists of these ingredients:

Communication

Both parties must be willing to engage in open, honest but *respectful* discourse. I've had plenty of people cross my path whom I just wanted to shake and scream in their faces, *"Quit being an asshole!"* That's honest and open, but it's not respectful *and* it may not necessarily be true. On more than a few occasions, I looked back at the incidents in question and realized I had it backwards.

they weren't the problem; *I* was the one being an asshole. When this happens, as it still does to this day although not nearly as much as it did in my younger days, I try to frame it in terms of a learning experience and a chance for self-improvement. What I say instead is, "I think we're working on different wavelengths here. Can we go over this again using different vocabulary?" I *invent* ways to bridge communication gaps instead of sabotaging them permanently in this way.

Enthusiastic consent

You cannot lead anyone who does not agree to your leadership. You won't get a thin dime out of someone who doesn't see the merit in your innovation. If you have less than enthusiastic consent before taking a potential sexual partner to bed, you're just begging for a sexual assault charge. Being a good leader, friend, partner and person means learning to seek out those people who are receptive to your overtures and stop wasting time on those who are not. Breaking someone's consent in any way can have severe and life-changing ramifications for everyone involved, as illustrated in the examples above.

Clarity

It doesn't make you stupid or overbearing to ask for or try to give greater clarification respectively when appropriate. In situations where your kneejerk reaction is to dismiss someone else as a jerk, you might try saying, "I'm not sure I understand where you're coming from. Can you explain it to me?" The business partner might be approached thus: "You seem like you're not entirely on board with this. Can you tell me why?" The friend may need to hear something like, "Hey, man, I know you've got a lot going on, but I need your input on something. Can I have a few minutes of floor time?" With regards to the romantic partner, you may say, "I get the feeling you really don't want to do this, and I respect that. Can we talk about it so I can understand you a little better?" All of these show respect, ask for clarification and don't "dumb down" the other person. It gives them the right to their thoughts and feelings while respectfully requesting access to them from the outside, with the understanding that they have every right to refuse. Of course, if such overtures are refused, it is time to reevaluate the relationship and determine if it's worth retaining.

Cooperation

Everyone in the relationship needs to be willing to cooperate to achieve mutual goals. Resistance or pushiness only begets more of the same until the immovable object and the irresistible force finally meet. In these situations, anyone with the most rudimentary understanding of physics knows that something has to give and it will usually do it at the worst possible time, in deference to the laws of Newton and Murphy respectively. Cooperation doesn't mean that one person always sets the tone or pace. A leader also knows when to step aside and let someone else take the initiative, whatever that may look like. However, cooperation doesn't mean setting aside your or someone else's right and obligation to give enthusiastic consent before moving forward.

You may be reading this and thinking, "What does this have to do with the brain, sixth sense or any of the rest of this gobbledygook he's hitting me over the head with?"

I'm glad you asked.

You see, communication is a two-way street, just as the Latin prefix co- implies, and each party has the right to continue communication only as long as both sides agree to continue it. We spoke earlier about the Master Mind and how everyone in it ideally is working toward the same goals and objectives. However, there is also a chance that at some point someone in the group may want or need the privacy of their own thoughts for a few minutes or possibly not consent to be in the group at all.

The physical signs of this, closed body language, curt responses, facial signals of anxiety, irritation or boredom, negative phrasing and so forth are all signs one should be looking for to help determine whether the Master Mind and its composite members are operating at their optimum potential. Open body language, excitement and interest, questions and relevant outbursts and an overall sense that "something else" is inhabiting the Master Mind's space at the same time and in sympathy with its goals are signals that everyone is present and engaged, consenting, clear and cooperating to achieve a unified goal.

This cannot, does not and will not happen without enthusiastic consent, period! It is simply *not* possible to achieve harmony where enthusiastic consent is not present. Lack of enthusiastic consent leads to the negative emotions we analyzed in the last chapter and will inevitably result in a situation where those emotions poison the well of the Master Mind. Developing the faculty of the sixth sense and applying *all* the capabilities of the brain to their utmost can help you avoid this pitfall and maintain an attitude that invites and encourages enthusiastic consent *without* violating someone else's lines, boundaries or "hard limits."

We've already determined that no one is universally great at everything. By getting a number of brains, subconscious minds, Infinite Intelligence access points and thoughts working on innovation simultaneously, success becomes nearly inevitable as long as the principle of "back to square one" is always kept in mind. It is the enthusiastic consent of all people involved that makes this possible, and when it happens, you will now know and recognize it for what it is.

Chapter Takeaways

1. The brain is set up to store, receive and *send* information.

2. We do not currently have the technology to even come close to replicating the complexity of the human brain.

3. The brain, subconscious, Ultimate Intelligence and sixth sense must work together, guided by human will, desire and need.

4. Before employing the sixth sense or the other capabilities of the mind, having the enthusiastic consent of the person or people on whom you intend to utilize it is imperative to success.

5. Communication, enthusiastic consent, clarification and cooperation are the hallmarks of a Master Mind functioning in true harmony and as required for the benefit of all.

*"There is only one thing that makes a
dream impossible to achieve:
the fear of failure."*

— Paulo Coelho, The Alchemist

14

Fear: The Innovator's
Greatest Stumbling Block

I've already mentioned that *Think and Grow Rich
for Inventors* is **not** *Think and Grow Rich*. While it
follows and applies Hill's basic principles and format,
there are places where I have deviated from the original
to lend greater relevance to the inventor over the pure
entrepreneur or businessman. This is not to take
anything away from either of these classes of people;
they have an important place in the global economy and
are needed badly. But this book is intended primarily to
apply those principles specifically as to the inventor and
to be read as a companion volume to Hill's original for

those who want to learn more about the entrepreneurial side of the ledger.

Because of this, I have taken some liberties with the format Hill used and drilled down in places he skimmed lightly and vice versa. The result, I hope, is a clearer and more easily understood version of Hill's opus that lends itself more readily to the inventor's worldview than that of the banker, CEO or financier. With this said, we move on to the topic of fear.

Fear is a survival mechanism at its most basic. It is fear that holds us back from jumping from high places or going swimming with alligators, keeps us paying our rent and taxes on time, leads us to avoid dangerous situations and warns us when something or someone is not working in our best interests. However, the overall purpose of fear is to protect us, not make us incapable of acting. Someone frozen with fear is an easy target for all manner of mischief, including ill thoughts, deeds and feelings, from sources internal and external to the person. Fear is an emotion, and every iteration of it occurs on a spectrum rather than a defined point.

Think of a color wheel for a visual aid for this. Negative emotions tend to blend together in endless variety, while positive emotions feel more or less the same. Knowing this, we can plot where we are on both the negative and positive spectra of emotion by identifying the degree to which our fears and positive desires influence our lives and then taking affirmative action to emphasize the traits we need and want while subverting or eliminating the ones we don't need or which do not aid us in our endeavors.

Just like everyone else, the inventor is subject to the Six Great Fears we discussed earlier. These fears are: Poverty, Criticism, Ill Health, Jealousy, Old Age and Death. Where these fears are present, only negative sentiment can grow. They literally "salt the fields" of the mind until all that can grow are negative, fearful emotions. Like always begets like, and these six fears, common to every person on the planet, attract thoughts and vibrations like themselves. This is the surest and fastest way to fail at anything!

Because of this, we need to create countermeasures against them in the same way a programmer might create a firewall that prohibits access to a computer program unless the proper entry protocols are employed. Therefore, it is best to start with what the fears are and for each, evaluate how this fear might be overcome to establish that each fear has an opposite number with which it can be effectively countered.

Poverty

Everyone knows someone who manages to live a reasonably happy life despite relative poverty, but I have never personally heard anyone living in poverty say they were fully content with their situation and don't even know anyone who knows anyone who knows anyone who has heard this. It is human nature to want "more." With "more" comes security...until "more" is attained. Then we look around and think we've arrived until we notice our house is too small, our car too old or not the right model, we don't belong to the "right" social clubs, we don't live in the "right" zip code, and so one. Fear of poverty or the *perception* of being impoverished is a powerful driver, but it is one that cannot yield positive results.

Counter

I am by no means saying anyone should embrace poverty, but I will argue it teaches some very powerful lessons. By taking an attitude that poverty is a relative and temporary condition which can be overcome by virtue of hard work, skill, education, talent and a little bit of luck (which if you've been paying attention you've already realized we can make for ourselves!) poverty is not something to be afraid of, but rather considered as a road bump. Venture capitalist James Altucher writes often of the fortune he lost in 2000 and how he managed to overcome it, moving from strength to strength despite his poverty and a lingering fear that someday poverty will return to his life. Despite this, he is aware that poverty is temporary unless we choose to give in to it and say, "This is it. This is my life." Instead, those who rise above poverty say, "This is my life *now*…but this will not *always* be my life, because I want something better and am willing to employ all my capabilities to bring it to pass."

Criticism

No one wants to look foolish or be seen to fail. Because of this, many people fear to make a move one way or the other on any matter. The scorn of one's peers is a powerful "freezing" force that makes us stop and question whether we're doing the right thing. While this is not altogether a bad thing, being the primary reason most people choose not to break the law, it can be an insurmountable barrier to the inventor's greatest gift: the ability to innovate.

Counter

Learning to evaluate criticism and the place from which it comes for its value is all-important and the *only* counter for criticism. People who criticize with good and honorable intentions, *coming from a place of knowledge and experience and with the other's best interests in mind*, are the only criticisms worth considering. Everyone else is speaking from their own fears in hopes, conscious or otherwise, of infecting you with them. By now, if you've been doing the exercises and working along with this book, you understand how to separate valid from invalid criticism. The key is not to not listen, but to refuse to act on criticism that isn't valid or applicable to you or your invention directly.

Ill Health

No one likes being sick. The late comedian George Carlin commented on the word "sick" and how unpleasant-sounding a word it is to describe an equally unpleasant condition. We fear ill health because we fear being less than we are capable of being, not to mention the fact that being sick in any aspect of our physical, mental or emotional health feels just as bad as the word "sick" sounds.

Counter

The only way to avoid ill health is to take proper care of ourselves. This is why doctors tell people to stop smoking, drink only in moderation, eat healthy foods in moderation and exercise. A healthy body leads to a healthy mind, while a healthy mind promotes a healthier body. Unless one is striving to compete in the Olympics, this doesn't have to be the focal point of one's life, but understand that healthier living creates of the body and mind a healthier organism that is more resistant to a wide spectrum of maladies of the body, mind, heart and soul.

Jealousy

There are two types of jealousy. The first is the kind associated with poverty, where we want "better" or "more" in the form of something someone else has. This may be a more attractive mate, a nicer car or house, bigger bank account and so on. The second kind of jealousy comes from a fear of losing what one has attained. This type of jealousy motivates the miser, the domineering partner, the kind of person who tells beggars on the street to "Get a job!" and the parent for whose children no one and nothing will ever be good enough in a bid to keep the children's affections.

Counter

The jealousy associated with poverty can be overcome in the same way as the greater fear of poverty itself. Simple, isn't it? The second kind of jealousy must be dealt with differently, because it requires understanding that what comes into one's life may not necessarily stay there. Money can be gained or lost in the blink of an eye. Partners may choose to leave or be taken from us by their will, accident, illness or death. Children whose parents are overbearing and determined that for their babies, only the best will do and they will remain damaged, weakened and overshadowed by their domineering parents forever, while those who grow strong despite this "helicopter parenting" will likely sever or severely limit contact once they reach adulthood. In both cases, the parent's worst fears concerning their children will be realized. By treating everything as precious while it is present without fear of losing it, it actually becomes more likely that not only will you overcome the fear known as jealousy, but will be able to keep and earn more of what you already have.

Old Age

Growing older is just a fact of life. The body starts to fail, we get wrinkles, we gain or lose a lot of weight, mental acuity begins to fade, we become less physically attractive and more concerned with the state of our hearts, souls and lifelong relationships. This is a common fear because who among us would not want to remain attractive, mentally clear and sharp and energetic until the day we die?

Counter

The best counter for the fear of aging is to appreciate that we learn and experience new things every day. We learn that the physical is not as important as the mental and emotional health of our being. We come to understand that physical beauty is transitory and by no means assured. We find out there are ways to keep our minds vibrant and healthy even into old age, where our experience and wisdom can gain its fullest expression and thus we have the most value to the coming generation. By understanding this and seeing the value of old age, rather than a process of slow decay, we acknowledge that aging demonstrates a far superior strength to anything the physical can provide: the power of influence over our world through the use of mind and heart.

Death

There is an old, sardonic saying that everybody wants to go to Heaven, but no one wants to die. This is absolutely true. No matter what our religious or intellectual convictions, fear of the Great Unknown is most readily represented by death. We understand the physiological process, but we have no idea what happens to the energy within us and the force of being we term a "soul" at the end of our lives, when the mechanisms that keep the soul intact in the body wither and fail. Fear of death is the ultimate universal negative drive.

Counter

The counter to the fear of death is to *live*. This sounds very simple and ironic, but I am absolutely serious. If you're going to die and you know this, why make your world a miserable place by fearing something that is inevitable? There are some people that find themselves sexually aroused at funerals, not because they have a morbid fascination with death but because sex is the opposite of that ultimate, final loneliness: It is something we share with another person and affirm in doing so that we are alive, we touch others' lives and are therefore worthy to continue living. However, simply locating a willing partner and having sex with them is not all it takes to overcome the fear of death. Supplanting that fear with something greater, like the fear of failing a loved one, not achieving everything one is capable of or living life in such a dishonorable way that no one wants to be around a given person are all useful ways to overcome the fear of death. In doing so, we remind ourselves to live while we're alive instead of waiting for a life after death that may or may not exist, and if it does may not automatically be granted to all for whatever reason. As Terry Goodkind wrote, "Your life is your own. Rise up and live it." You may die, of course. You may fail. But is that better than fearing something that you cannot avoid, because like it or not, it *will* happen to you and everyone you know sooner or later?

—

Someone did a survey of people in retirement homes facing the end of their lives. They asked about what sorts of things they would have changed and what they regretted. The number one regret of people at the end of their days on Earth are the things they wish they would have done. It was never "I shouldn't have done this" or "I wish I hadn't done that." It was always the things that someone didn't do. "I wish I would have spent more time with my family." "I wish I had taken that dream trip instead of canceling at the last minute to work." "I wish I would have written a book or built that idea." All of these answers, one way or the other, reflect the regret of a moment or life when one thing was chosen over another because of *fear*.

If you continue on the course you're on now, will you have those regrets when you're 80 or 90? What could you be building right now that will let you live a life you love? Imagine never building that thing you have in mind right now. What feelings might you have if that thing is left undone?

You have the power. You can get the knowledge. All that's left is action. But to take that action, two more things remain to be discussed: the excuses we make for our failures, also known as alibis, and self-evaluation to determine where to go from here.

Hill observed fifty-five (*yes, 55!*) different alibis that unsuccessful people used to cover up their failures by blaming something or someone else for their misfortune. As innovators, we don't have that option. If it doesn't work, it doesn't work because we didn't *make* it work. Remember Edison and 10,000 tries at making a lightbulb for a powerful illustration of this. To say anything else, pardon the expression, is pure, unadulterated bullshit. In fact, it is of *less* value than bullshit, because you can at least use bullshit to fertilize your lawn and make grass grow. What can you grow that's tangible, useful or good with the kind of bullshit you feed yourself to create an alibi for failure?

Hill expressed these so clearly and so precisely that I am reprinting them here exactly as he presented them. As you read each, see if you can evaluate the fears and negative emotions from which each arises and how each one can be overcome. This will become important in the next chapter, so pay attention!

Napoleon Hill's 55 Alibis for Failure

1. IF I didn't have a wife and family . . .

2. IF I had enough "pull" . . .

3. IF I had money . . .

4. IF I had a good education . . .

5. IF I could get a job . . .

6. IF I had good health . . .

7. IF I only had time . . .

8. IF times were better . . .

9. IF other people understood me . . .

10. IF conditions around me were only different . . .

11. IF I could live my life over again . . .

12. IF I did not fear what "*they*" would say . . .

13. IF I had been given a chance . . .

14. IF I now had a chance . . .

15. IF other people didn't "have it in for me" . . .

16. IF nothing happens to stop me . . .

17. IF I were only younger . . .

18. IF I could only do what I want . . .

19. IF I had been born rich . . .

20. IF I could meet "the right people" . . .

21. IF I had the talent that some people have . . .

22. IF I dared assert myself . . .

23. IF I only had embraced past opportunities . . .

24. IF people didn't get on my nerves . . .

25. IF I didn't have to keep house and look after the children . . .

26. IF I could save some money . . .

27. IF the boss only appreciated me . . .

28. IF I only had somebody to help me . . .

29. IF my family understood me . . .

30. IF I lived in a big city . . .

31. IF I could just get started . . .

32. IF I were only free . . .

33. IF I had the personality of some people . . .

34. IF I were not so fat . . .

35. IF my talents were known . . .

36. IF I could just get a "break" . . .

37. IF I could only get out of debt . . .

38. IF I hadn't failed . . .

39. IF I only knew how . . .

40. IF everybody didn't oppose me . . .

41. IF I didn't have so many worries . . .

42. IF I could marry the right person . . .

43. IF people weren't so dumb . . .

44. IF my family were not so extravagant . . .

45. IF I were sure of myself . . .

46. IF luck were not against me . . .

47. IF I had not been born under the wrong star . . .

48. IF it were not true that "what is to be will be" . . .

49. IF I did not have to work so hard . . .

50. IF I hadn't lost my money . . .

51. IF I lived in a different neighborhood . . .

52. IF I didn't have a "past" . . .

53. IF I only had a business of my own . . .

54. IF other people would only listen to me . . .

55. IF I had the courage to see myself as I really am, I would find out what is wrong with me, and correct it, then I might have a chance to profit by my mistakes and learn something from the experience of others, for I know that there is something

wrong with me, or I would now be where *I would have been if* I had spent more time analyzing my weaknesses, and less time building alibis to cover them.

Study this list carefully and avoid the phrasing *or intent* of these alibis. Thoughts becomes actions. Actions become habits. Make sure your habits of thought, word and deed build toward success.

The Universe is listening.

Chapter Takeaways

1. There are six great fears common to every person: poverty, criticism, ill health, jealousy, old age and death.

2. These fears can be countered.

3. Of the 55 alibis for failure, all of them link back to at least one and in many cases several of the six great fears which drive the seven negative emotions discussed earlier in this book.

4. Thoughts become actions. Actions become habits. Bad habits can only lead to poor outcomes.

*"The first and best victory is to conquer
self. To be conquered by self is, of all
things, the most shameful and vile."*

— Plato

15

Self-Evaluation

This book is intended as a blueprint for self-mastery first and foremost. *You cannot master anything or anyone else, nor can you achieve your full potential, if you cannot control your thoughts, feelings or actions and your responses to those of others.*

Knowing this, and drawing upon the information presented in this book, it is your turn to put these things into conscious action, if you have not done so already. In order to do this, of course, you need a plan.

For this reason, I have included a self-evaluation similar to the one Napoleon Hill created at the end of *Think and Grow Rich*, with a few additions and revisions. If you have already read that book and used this questionnaire to plot your progress, few of the questions should come as a surprise to you. If you have not, then you will find this invaluable in helping you to self-assess and start on the road to ongoing reevaluation of yourself, your thinking and your goals.

This is not a timed test and there are no wrong answers. The only way you can fail here is not to answer these questions with complete self-awareness and honesty or to refuse to answer at all. Remember, this is for your own benefit and development in charting your progress through the techniques and skills taught in this book. I'm A professor; I'm not *your* professor, except insofar as you have decided to read this book and apply the information inside. I'm not grading you on your answers; the only person who really needs to know the answers to these questions is *you*.

1. What do you believe it means to be an innovator?

2. What do you believe it means to be an inventor?

3. What have you done *today* to make your innovation or invention a reality?

4. Have you sought out any help to make your innovation or invention a reality?

5. Do you complain often of "feeling bad," and if so, what is the cause?

6. Do you find fault with other people at the slightest provocation?

7. Do you frequently make mistakes in your work, and if so, why?

8. Are you sarcastic and offensive in your conversation?

9. Do you deliberately avoid the association of anyone, and if so, why?

10. Do you suffer frequently with indigestion? If so, what is the cause?

11. Does life seem futile and the future hopeless to you? If so, why?

12. Do you like your occupation? If not, why?

13. Do you often feel self-pity, and if so why?

14. Are you envious of those who excel you?

15. To which do you devote most time, thinking of *success*, or of *failure*?

16. Are you gaining or losing self-confidence as you grow older?

17. Do you learn something of value from all mistakes? Are you permitting some relative or acquaintance to worry you? If so, why?

18. Are you sometimes "in the clouds" and at other times in the depths of despondency?

19. Who has the most inspiring influence upon you? What is the cause?

20. Do you tolerate negative or discouraging influences which you can avoid?

21. Are you careless of your personal appearance? If so, when and why?

22. Have you learned how to "drown your troubles" by being too busy to be annoyed by them?

23. Would you call yourself a "spineless weakling" if you permitted others to do your thinking for you?

24. Do you neglect taking time for personal mental hygiene and health until you become ill-tempered and irritable?

25. How many preventable disturbances annoy you, and why do you tolerate them?

26. Do you resort to liquor, narcotics, or cigarettes to "quiet your nerves"? If so, why do you not try will-power instead?

27. Does anyone "nag" you, and if so, for what reason?

28. Do you have a *definite major purpose*, and if so, what is it, and what plan have you for achieving it?

29. Do you suffer from any of the Six Basic Fears? If so, which ones?

30. Have you a method by which you can shield yourself against the negative influence of others?

31. Do you make deliberate use of auto-suggestion to make your mind positive?

32. Which do you value most, your material possessions, or your privilege of controlling your own thoughts?

33. Are you easily influenced by others, against your own judgment?

34. Has today added anything of value to your stock of knowledge or state of mind?

35. Do you face squarely the circumstances which make you unhappy, or sidestep the responsibility?

36. Do you analyze all mistakes and failures and try to profit by them or, do you take the attitude that this is not your duty?

37. Can you name three of your most damaging weaknesses?

38. What are you doing to correct them?

39. Do you encourage other people to bring their worries to you for sympathy?

40. Do you choose, from your daily experiences, lessons or influences which aid in your personal advancement?

41. Does your presence have a negative influence on other people as a rule?

42. What habits of other people annoy you most?

43. Do you form your own opinions or permit yourself to be influenced by other people?

44. Have you learned how to create a mental state of mind with which you can shield yourself against all discouraging influences?

45. Does your occupation inspire you with faith and hope?

46. Are you conscious of possessing spiritual forces of sufficient power to enable you to keep your mind free from all forms of *fear*?

47. Does your religious or philosophical belief structure help you to keep your own mind positive? If not, why?

48. Do you feel it your duty to share other people's worries? If so, why?

49. If you believe that "birds of a feather flock together" what have you learned about yourself by studying the friends whom you attract?

50. What connection, if any, do you see between the people with whom you associate most closely, and any unhappiness you may experience?

51. Could it be possible that some person whom you consider to be a friend is, in reality, your worst enemy, because of his negative influence on your mind?

52. By what rules do you judge who is helpful and who is damaging to you?

53. Are your intimate associates mentally superior or inferior to you?

54. How much time out of every 24 hours do you devote to:
    a. your occupation
    b. sleep
    c. play and relaxation
    d. acquiring useful knowledge
    e. plain waste

55. Who among your acquaintances,
    a. encourages you most
    b. cautions you most
    c. discourages you most
    d. helps you most in other ways?

56. What is your greatest worry? Why do you tolerate it?

57. When others offer you free, unsolicited advice, do you accept it without question, or analyze their motive?

58. What, above all else, do you most *desire?* Do you intend to acquire it? Are you willing to subordinate all other desires for this one? How much time daily do you devote to acquiring it?

59. Do you change your mind often? If so, why?

60. Do you usually finish everything you begin?

61. Are you easily impressed by other people's business or professional titles, college degrees, or wealth?

62. Are you easily influenced by what other people think or say of you?

63. Do you cater to people because of their social or financial status?

64. Whom do you believe to be the greatest person living? In what respect is this person superior to yourself?

65. How much time have you devoted to studying and answering these questions?

66. Did anything you answered in this survey surprise you when you thought about or revisited it after the fact the first time or at any other time?

67. Do you feel like you understand your mind, motivations and drives better?

68. Name eight people this month, two per week, whom you would like to integrate into your Master Mind.

69. For each of these people, name one quality they have that would benefit you and your plans, and one quality you have that would benefit them and theirs.

70. How would you approach each of these people?

Hill recommended doing this once a week, but I think it is both more revealing and less like a chore to do this once a month. Choose one day each month during which you can sit down and work on this questionnaire without interruption. I say each month because it gives you more time to work on the important business of innovating and building your Master Mind, as well as more insight into how you're progressing when you see it in larger chunks. Small, incremental steps, or as James Altucher puts it, trying to improve your life by 1% each day, is more likely to establish solid, lasting change than being committed for a week and walking away.

By revisiting and reevaluating your answers, you can not only see how you have progressed to this point but map out your progression plan for the future. If you wish, you can present this to your Master Mind for them to work on as well, so everyone knows everyone's minds and progress. Some may not be receptive to this, and that's fine. However, if they won't share their minds with you now, it is not reasonable to expect they will when the stakes are higher later on.

*"The end is in the beginning
and lies far ahead."*

— Ralph Ellison

16

Closing Thoughts

This book has been many years in the making for me. I started thinking about it while I was still at Fish & Neave and wishing I could find the time to make it a reality. Almost two decades later, I finally followed Napoleon Hill's advice and instead of waiting for it to happen, took the steps I needed to *make* it happen.

After writing this book and revisiting *Think and Grow Rich* with the new eyes required to apply its principles to the spirit of invention rather than pure capitalism, I've come to realize that every time I got off track with my plans or hesitated in their execution, it is because

I was giving in to fear and alibis. I was literally *giving myself permission to fail* before I ever even got off the ground. Only when I read an exceedingly vulgar email telling me quite literally that I "don't have the balls" that I made the conscious decision to give myself permission to succeed.

And I did.

Although Fish & Neave helped make me what I am today, I knew my background and lack of an Ivy League law school education would inevitably hold me back there. I was determined to make it based upon my own merits and to me that meant not having a "boss" that sat in judgment of my work. I never forgot the lessons I learned, however, and promised never to judge anyone's potential by what they had done in the past. Everyone has a right to prove their worth through their hard work. I remembered this when we were interviewing for our first paralegal. I have never forgotten it and it is my approach in hiring even today.

As you may remember from earlier in this book or as retold in full in *Escaping the Gray*, I got needled pretty badly with jokes about leaving Fish & Neave to go out on my own. "We'll keep your resume on file...you'll be back!" "There are no inventors in Florida!" "Why don't they invent a voting machine in Florida so they don't have 'hanging chads?'" "Where's the stability in your own law firm?"

The last statement took on a certain dark humor in 2004.

Fish & Neave decided to close its doors and its assets were bought by a general practice law firm, Ropes & Gray. Talking about lack of stability, Ropes & Gray weathered a slew of desertions by top partners and associates in the wake of the merger. Fish & Neave is now a footnote in history. Never again will it be the powerhouse firm that represented the Wright Brothers, Bell, Edison, Ford and their ilk. I was sad to see them fall, but appreciated the irony in their cocksure certainty that I'd come back on bended knee. Even so, I wished them nothing but the best. Just because I was a fish out of water and a youngster with too much ambition and not enough restraint on it didn't mean it was a bad place. It just wasn't a good fit for me, and I still wonder how some of my old colleagues are getting on from time to time.

By watching modern inventors and studying the stories of the giants, I learned that my mind works much like the inventor's does. I have my own brand of innovation that I bring to the table, but I certainly wouldn't put myself on the same plane as the guy who invented the java sleeve, never mind Edison et al. I am more interested in being the midwife to innovation than its architect, helping bring it from the drawing board to life. This is my niche and my life's work, and I'm comfortable with and rewarded well by knowing that I am exactly where I'm supposed to be and doing exactly what I'm supposed to do.

These are some things I've learned which may have been neglected elsewhere in this book, but that I think are important enough to be discussed before I leave you to your pursuit of whatever goals you have.

Inventors do not ask permission to invent. They simply proceed. Those who do ask permission invariably get left behind while someone else gets to the Patent Office and the prize first.

Inventors must be mavericks. They don't follow the status quo. They ask scary questions like "Why?" and "Why not?" that give false leaders and those who rely on "authority" more than leadership indigestion and insomnia.

Inventors see the world differently than others. They imagine. They create. And then they do it all over again.

Inventors create fortune for themselves and others by virtue of their innovation.

Inventors do not back down from challenge, embracing it instead as opportunity.

Inventors maintain the courage of their convictions that their innovations can and will make the world better than they found it.

I've always admired the inventive spirit. The innovator, the entrepreneur and the inventor are all heroes of mine, no matter how trivial or mundane their achievements may seem. For every one of these people who has successfully created something, there are a thousand, even ten thousand, who sit around and bemoan the fact that they haven't. I wanted to create something, a place where the small inventor could find advice, counsel and help...and I did it.

But I had to overcome a healthy dose of the Six Great Fears to do so.

Even worse, some of the criticism and mockery I'd taken had gotten under my skin. What if I failed? What would Saba and my children say? How would they feel about me? I can tolerate just about anything except failure and being an object of pity. If my plans went horribly awry, would I lose them forever along with my own sense of self-worth?

Like hell I will, I thought.

I've been honored to work directly with some amazing inventors and entrepreneurs in my practice, people who made themselves and others rich beyond Croesus's most fevered dreams with their innovations. I have had the distinct privilege of guiding others through the labyrinthine requirements of patent law and inspiring a few to take up shingles in this field as well through my adjunct professorship at Nova Southeastern University Law School. I've built and kept a Master Mind that has served me well for two decades and counting, and am fortunate to count my best friends in its ranks.

If you have stuck with me this far, I hope you have had some insights into yourself and that these insights have sparked a plan for how you can proceed to implement them into good, actionable habits. Even if you haven't, that doesn't mean the time was wasted; it simply means you haven't found the way forward *yet*.

But your day will come. Plan your work and work your plan, and success will be as inevitably as the sun rising tomorrow. You may not be able to see it because of cloud cover or being inside, but that doesn't mean the sun isn't there.

Success is the same, and it's waiting for you to come find it.

I wish you luck, happy inventing and fortune in your endeavors to come!

About the Author

Every great idea and successful invention starts with a dream.

From his earliest days as an engineer, John Rizvi dreamed of working with inventors and entrepreneurs of all stripes. He set his sights on the premier patent law firm in the nation; a firm that counted Bell, Edison, the Wright Brothers and Ford among its distinguished list of clients. Between his hard work, determination and willingness to take risks, he succeeded, rising through the ranks at the firm.

But success came with a price. Instead of helping innovators, he found himself spending most of his time with in-house lawyers of large, institutional and corporate clients—far removed from the inventor and the creative spark of a new idea that makes it all possible.

JOHN RIZVI, ESQ.

A fateful encounter on his way to work one day forced him to look at his life in a different way and commit to taking the chance of a lifetime...or watching it fade away forever. With the backing of friends, mentors and his beloved wife, John found the courage to pursue his dream of founding a law firm focused solely on protecting new ideas.

John Rizvi discovered the power of Napoleon Hill's seminal work, *Think and Grow Rich*, while studying engineering in college. Later, while in law school and then as an attorney, the lessons he learned from this landmark book showed him the way forward when he felt hopelessly lost.

Upon learning that *Think and Grow Rich* had passed into the public domain, John acquired a new dream. He decided to write his own version, tooled specifically for his own personal heroes: the men and women who innovate, create and reshape our world every day, in ways large and small. He presents it here in *Think and Grow Rich for Inventors*.

To learn more about John Rivzi, visit www.ThePatentProfessor.com

Bibliography

Bandell, Brian. "The Big Payoff: Med School Dropout Sells Startup for $100M" *Upstart Business Journal.* http://upstart. bizjournals.com/entrepreneurs/hot-shots/2014/04/11/ alexander-gomez-new-wave-surgical.html Web. Accessed 9/26/2016.

Ghose, Tia. "Supercomputer Takes 40 Minutes to Model 1 Second of Brain Activity" *LiveScience.* http://www.livescience. com/42561-supercomputer-models-brain-activity.html Web. Accessed 9/26/2016.

Heinlein, Robert A. *Starship Troopers.* New York: Putnam, 1959. Print.

Hill, Napoleon. *Think and Grow Rich.* No. Hollywood, CA: Melvin Powers, Wilshire Book, 1966. Print.

Kraig, Donald Michael. *Modern Magick: Twelve Lessons in the High Magickal Arts.* 2nd ed. St. Paul, MN: Llewellyn Publications, 2010. Print.

Newell, Jim. "The IRS Is More Than Four Time More Popular Than Congress" *Gawker.* http://gawker.com/5860272/the-irs-is-more-than-four-times-more-popular-than-congress .Web. Accessed 9/26/2016.

Rizvi, John. *Escaping the Gray*. Miami: TheIdeaAttorneys.com, 2016. E-book.

Sheffield, Toria. "Nikola Tesla Was a Virgin with OCD who Fell in Love with a Pigeon" *History Buff*. http://historybuff.com/4-strange-facts-about-nikola-tesla-to-share-at-your-next-nerd-gathering-6Q0pA9jgDgao Web. Accessed 9/26/2016.

Wells, Ed. "To Serve & Protect Compared" *CNN Money*. http://money.cnn.com/magazines/fsb/fsb_archive/2001/11/01/312461/ Web. Accessed 9/26/2016.

Zimmerman Jones, Andrew, nd. "Power" *About Education*. http://physics.about.com/od/glossary/g/power.htm Web. Accessed 9/26/2016.

CPSIA information can be obtained
at www.ICGtesting.com
Printed in the USA
FSHW020651160421